WHAT DO[ES IT MEAN TO REL]AX?

Before we talk about how to relax, we need to better understand what it means to relax. The mistake we most commonly make is thinking that relaxing is synonymous with sleeping or with some state of dulled awareness.

Relaxing is something we do while we are wide awake.

Even more to the point, relaxation is a skill to be acquired and used while we are still at work. I am convinced that those who think of relaxation as something that is best done off the firing line of life miss the point. Real relaxation skills are those that can be practiced in the midst of the stress of life.

RELAXATION
FOR
CHRISTIANS

H. Newton Malony, Ph.D.

BALLANTINE BOOKS • NEW YORK

Copyright © 1992 by Dr. H. Newton Malony

All rights reserved under International and Pan-American Copyright Conventions. Published in the United States of America by Ballantine Books, a division of Random House, Inc., New York, and simultaneously in Canada by Random House of Canada Limited, Toronto.

Library of Congress Catalog Card Number: 92-90142

ISBN 0-345-36649-2

Manufactured in the United States of America

First Edition: August 1992

93109

Table of Contents

I am convinced that the most important
question of the '90s will be,
"What does it mean to be spiritual?"
—BILL MOYERS

Prologue

In introducing his book *A Little Exercise for Young Theologians*, Martin Marty said that it was like greeting cards sent to new, tried, and tired theologians.

You might see this book on relaxation as a set of greeting cards sent to new, tried, and tired Christians—or as an "invitation to the party" to Christians who are party goers but haven't quite caught the knack of easeful enjoyment of the Christian experience.

Relaxation for Christians is a "bon voyage" card sent to first-time travelers who have decided to relax and who have their bags already packed, ready to get on board.

It is a "happy anniversary" card for those who have tried relaxing for the past year or more and want to go on for a "relaxation black belt."

And it is a "get well" card for old-timers who once knew the joy of relaxation but have forgotten to practice their skill and have become tense again.

1

Becoming and remaining a relaxed person should be a goal for every one of those Christians and for others who don't fit any of the greeting-card categories just noted.

To relax is an instinct, a talent, a skill, and a gift—all at the same time. Let me show you what I mean.

Relaxation is a natural *instinct*. We humans were made to let go and slow down. Our natural state is an alertness that is calm and peaceful, alternating with trustful, restorative sleep. We were not created for the too-wide-awake striving that makes us feel stressed and war-torn.

Relaxation is a *talent*. Some people seem to do it better than others. Some folk take to relaxing, as to art or music, more easily than others. For those others, tension seems to come with the territory.

However, relaxation is also a *skill*. It can be taught. It can be learned. It can be practiced. It can be improved. Training can overcome lack of talent. Training can reawaken the instinct to relax.

Most importantly for Christians, relaxation is a *gift*. It is free for the asking. Better said, it is free for the *taking*. It costs nothing, but it must be grasped. It is the gift of faith. Nine times in the gospels, Jesus said "Be not anxious." There was probably no other prohibition he repeated more often. Eleven times he pronounced the opposite of anxiety, namely "peace." In John 14:27, he sums it up with these words: "Peace I leave with you; my peace I give unto you; not as the world gives to you. Let not your hearts be troubled, neither let them be afraid." Jesus goes to the heart of the matter. Tension and stress are signs that we are afraid. Living the relaxed life is possible because of God's gift of peace, which calms our fears.

This is a book of hope. Take it as an unexpected greeting card you have received in the mail. Whether you are an unconverted stress-and-strainer, a novice relaxer, a veteran practitioner of the art, or a tired old-timer needing a relaxation transfusion, this book is meant for you.

I have tried to write in a user-friendly manner, to borrow a computer term. Like a computer, this book offers much but promises nothing. You will get nothing out of it unless you start with some anticipation. Hopefully, it will be more than "garbage in, garbage out."

Each chapter is short. The examples are true-to-life. The exercises are practical. You can put the content to work for you day by day. Like the BMW automobile ad states about its cars, this book is intended to be "a way to survive in a hostile world." Who knows, you may catch the spirit. That is my hope.

A final thought: Relax—here, now, right at this moment while you are reading these words. It is my intention that you read on "relaxingly." Relaxing should not become the latest project you take on to become perfect. If that happens, this book will have failed. It will have become simply the latest way Christians can struggle to achieve a "works righteousness"—in an ever-so-subtle manner. Unfortunately many books on relaxation do just that. They leave people more stressed than when they began. Not this one, I hope. If and when you feel yourself becoming tense, put the book down! Better still, throw it away! Let this book relax you as you read it; else its purpose is defeated. I wish you well on your relaxation journey. I look forward to seeing you on the trail!

CHAPTER 1

The Age of Anxiety

The first half of the twentieth century was a time of fear. The second half could be called the age of anxiety. My father, who died in 1937, knew a lot about fear. He knew almost nothing about anxiety. He almost made it through the Great Depression before he died. In his struggle to survive it, there were days when he did not know whether he would be able to buy a loaf of bread. Meat and vegetables were rare. Those years were quite a comedown for a man who owned a construction company that built huge apartment buildings in Birmingham, Alabama, before the crash of 1929!

However, I doubt my father knew what blood pressure was. He didn't have time for hypertension. He was too busy surviving. He died from pneumonia, not from stress or strain. Like British citizens during the German blitzkrieg of the Second World War, my father didn't have time to worry about his health.

4

Not so his son. I don't recall ever lacking meat and vegetables, much less bread! Although I was born in the middle of the depression, I never knew it existed. My father faced the fear for me. He protected me from the dread about whether there would be food for the next meal. We were poor, but I did not know it. We were in desperate straits, but I did not feel it. He was too strong and too proud to let me know his fear.

After his death, when I was six, my mother continued my father's custom. She kept her fear to herself. There was much to frighten this new widow. Left with no home, no insurance, and no skill for making money, she must have known true terror. All she had was good health and a helpless child. Yes, fear must have been her close and constant companion—but she never introduced me to that unwelcome acquaintance.

No, my problem has not been survival. I am the stereotypical child of the second half of the twentieth century. My problem has been anxiety, not fear. My companions have been stress and strain, those two esses most of us know only too well. Like those modern women who want to "have it all," as they perceive many men do, I, too, have not been satisfied with just being average. I have wanted to make it and to take it—whatever "it" has been at a given time in my life. I have yearned to be more than the most, better than the best, know more than the knowers, and be richer than the rich. I often have said, "I wish the day had thirty-six hours in it; then maybe I could do what I want to do!" I have been trying to assuage my anxiety over not achieving, not banish a fear of not surviving.

I am a child of the post-1950s. As one bard said, "This is the age of *compression*." I know what he meant. I am anxious. I am stretched. I am stressed. I am strained. I am exhausted. I am confused. I have hypertension. I am worried. I feel dissatisfied. I am restless. I feel incomplete. I feel compressed—into too short a time, too many demands, too few rewards, too frequent frustrations, too many dissatisfactions.

My predicament came home to me recently. A young woman asked me, "Do you always have that deep line in your forehead between your eyes? You look worried." I had to admit to her I didn't know I had such an obvious line on my face. I did not realize my tension showed to others. I did not realize I was worried. But I must have been. What made matters even worse was that this young woman made her comment to me at a coffee hour just after I had given a church talk on "peace of mind"!

One survey said that one in four of us suffers from this syndrome of worry, dissatisfaction, stress, anxiety, and compression. I am convinced the figure is much higher. We rush from one task to another, from one relationship to another. We make desperate attempts to compress more into our lives than any humans who have ever lived before. No, I am not the exception. I'm not just one out of four. I may even be nearer to representing four out of four. I have many brothers and sisters; you may be among them.

I travel to many places. Often I look out the window of a plane and see cities dotting the landscape. More often than not, I do not know the city names or any of the people who live their lives along those streets that stretch out like patterned quilts across the landscape. However, I believe those people are like you and me. We are all one of a kind—human beings all. We are tension-tempted, stress-filled. That is what it means to live in the second half of the twentieth century, an age of great tension and strain.

Many of us could probably identify with the dream one

man had in which there were fires all over his backyard. He tried to put them out with a garden hose. But he failed. No sooner did he put out one fire than another would crop up nearby. They just kept erupting, no matter how hard he tried. He was simply not powerful enough to put them all out.

Like that dreamer, many folk have realized that something was out of kilter in their lives. They have tried to slow down, gain control, and stop the madness that engulfs them. Yet, the compulsions to get all they can and to never lose control are like fires that keep erupting randomly in the backyards of their lives. They can't seem to get ahead of the game. The demands of the day and a not-too-subtle habit of trying to do it all seduce them back into the frantic state they were trying to avoid.

We "human torches" need help. We need to learn how to relax and back off from obsessive activity and frantic overcontrol. Not only have we been unable to put out old fires before new fires erupt, but we may in fact be compulsive neurotics who start them in the first place. Victims we may not be. Perpetrators we may well be.

Oh, I admit that sometimes I behave admirably. I take control of my stress and calm myself down on rare occasions. I remember missing a flight from Detroit to Denver. I had to take a later flight. Because of this delay, I knew I would miss an important appointment. On top of this, I got assigned to a window seat on a crowded 737 aircraft, much to my displeasure. Being six feet tall with long legs to boot, I felt like a sardine forced into a can. I avoid window seats like the plague. Fortunately for me this was one of those few times when I talked some sense into myself. Had I not reminded myself to relax and quit obsessing about being hemmed in on a two-hour flight, I would have been constantly twisting in my seat, looking around for empty spaces, casting hostile glares toward those around me who I felt were intruding on my space. In other words, I would have tried to change the unchangeable. Fortunately I was writing this book at that time, and I decided to practice what I was recommending. I relaxed and enjoyed the trip—in spite of a teenager's seeming compulsion in the seat in front of me to put his seat back as far as it would go and jam my knees!

Most of us don't fly that often. So perennial airline delays, stand-by seating, lost luggage, and the atrocities of cold entrées and even colder stewardesses (such as are absent from Alaska Airlines' flights according to their ads) are infrequent enough for us to take them in stride. It's those far more routine jammed-up-knees incidents in which I, and, I suspect, you, could probably use the most assistance. I was glad I could talk myself into calming down on the flight from Detroit to Denver, but what I really want is to remain calm on Monday through Friday, when the going gets tight on the ground rather than in the air.

Like a lot of people, I'm pretty good at being "Mr. Calm" when my schedule is uncrowded and manageable. But I can easily be tempted to "max out" under the pressure of too many things to do or too many plans gone askew. On some of these occasions I don't do well. I become fragmented, frazzled, and forgetful. After it's all over, I sometimes wish that there had been someone who had grabbed me by the shoulders and jerked me into realizing what I was doing to myself. "See here," I would have them say, "calm down, relax. Take this problem a step at a time. You'll do a better job if you don't get so anxious and upset."

There is danger in this kind of everyday tension. As we will see in more detail in a later chapter, too much stress can wear us down as surely as too much fat in the diet can clog our arteries. Tight muscles become prematurely constricted. Arthritis can result. Hypertension can cause ulcers, headaches, allergies, heart attacks—you name it. It can happen.

It can slip up on a person. About twenty years ago, in the months after my mother died, I discovered that I had elevated blood pressure. I suspect I had the problem before that. Mother died when we were making a major move, from Tennessee to California; it couldn't have happened at a worse time. However, I believe that her death was simply the occasion that pushed my stress over the line. The high blood pressure was but the tip of a tension iceberg that finally reared its ugly head above the ocean of my life. Like many other people, I had needed to learn how to relax long before I realized I was tense. There is no question in my mind that I had been, and probably still am, a Type A person, out to achieve as much as possible in as short a time as possible. I've been fighting this problem of hypertension ever since the day I learned I had it. I partially control it by diet and exercise, but knowing how to truly, consistently, relax still eludes me.

I guess you could say that this chapter is partly "true confession time" for me. I intended this book to read as though I wrote it for myself. But always, my hope has been that, in making it real for me, I will also have hit upon the surest way to make it real for you. When I speak to myself, my guess is that my experience is your experience, in essence if not in specific details. You've been in tight places on airplanes. You've tried hard and failed. You've become confused in the midst of frantic schedules and overcommitments. You've suddenly realized your tension has turned into symptoms.

If you doubt that this book is written to you, check it out.

Below are some common situations in which folk get stressed out. See how many ring a bell with your experience. Put a check by the ones that you have experienced.

- You have a flat tire on the way to pick up your children from school. ( )

- You forget an appointment to have your teeth cleaned. ( )

- You burn the vegetables while studying for an exam. ( )

- You get caught in traffic on the freeway after a long workday. ( )

- You hurry off late to your job after a sleepless night of sickness. ( )

- You accidentally make two dates for the same evening. ( )

- You get invited to be a club officer during a year of many other commitments. ( )

- You get up early to prepare a speech you'd intended to work on yesterday. ( )

- You read your Bible and pray for guidance but blow up when something goes wrong at work. ( )

- You rush to the bank during lunch hour and have to wait in a long line. ( )

- You want to buy another car but have to work overtime to do it. ( )

- You get bounced from an overbooked airline flight. ( )

- You have to attend a family funeral during a busy work season. ( )

- You stay up past midnight packing for a business trip you must take the next day. ( )

- You have an argument with your spouse over bills the same evening you host one of your church's covenant group meetings. ( )

- You have to rush to pick up a child from swimming, prepare supper, and get to another child's recital. ( )

- You get into bed and your spouse wants to make love after you've spent a long day straining to get everything done. ( )

- You work long hours: You come home after your children are in bed and must leave again before they get up the next morning. ( )

- Your spouse wants you to spend the day at the beach just after you have come back from a business trip. ( )

- You have to work two jobs to buy the house you want. ( )

- Your children want to go to an expensive private school. ( )

- You want to be a faithful Christian and the pastor asks you to teach church school. ( )

- Your father dies and you are the executor of his will. ( )

- You want to attend night school while working full-time. ( )

- Your child wants you to join the Girl Scout (or Boy Scout) committee. ( )

- Somebody else gets the promotion you've worked for. ( )

- The person you are dating steadily tells you he or she wants to go out with others. ( )

- You get a call at home to return to your work after an already long workday on a night when you have other plans. ( )

- You are asked to give a large donation to the church. ( )

- Your child is injured in an automobile accident. ( )

- You find your house needs a new roof. ( )

- Your spouse dies. ( )

- You stay up after midnight on Christmas Eve just getting all the presents and goodies ready for the next day. ( )

- You make mistakes at a recital. ( )

- You get a bad cold the day before an important meeting. ( )

Did your mere reading of that list leave you feeling in need of a vacation, or at the very least a walk around the block? You likely spent little of your imagination in placing yourself in more than a few of these predicaments. They and their like are our common lot. And when more than one stressor visits within a short period of time, we really feel compressed and overextended. Each new frustration adds up, and we may begin to feel like a time bomb waiting to explode with the next demand.

You noticed that several of the stress-inducing situations involve religion? I suspect that in spite of our best intentions, a good number of the occasions for our tension revolve around church. Further, many of us Christians have not found any real help from our faith with our anxiety and stress. We feel guilty if we do not live up to church demands or to sermons that condemn us. We need to admit that. What should be a cure has become part of the problem.

Now, this lack of help from our religion may come from our not having listened to what the preacher said. It may also come from our not reading the Scriptures thoroughly enough. However, I think most of us would confess that, often, what we hear and read makes us feel more uncomfortable and restless than relaxed and calm. The church always seems to be demanding more and more of our time, money, and energy. Being Christian in our day may aggravate rather than help the problem.

Following Jesus in the late twentieth century is not easy. We are taught to respond to God's love by (1) taking up a cross, (2) studying the Bible daily, (3) praying at all times, (4) telling others about their need for God, (5) resisting the temptation to do evil, (6) being kind to our neighbors, (7) living holy lives in a secular world, and (8) avoiding overindulgence while others suffer. And this list does not even include the requirements that Christians should love one another and be like their Master and "go about doing good."

Christianity requires a tremendous amount of devotion from its followers. To do all that faith in Jesus requires in an age of stress and strain requires a great amount of energy. I heard of one church that required its members to live within three miles of the church building so that they could attend

morning prayer meetings at least four times a week before
work or school. The membership vows of another church
require its adherents to state publicly that they will be loyal
to that particular fellowship and uphold it with their prayers,
their presence, their gifts, and their service. And as if this
were not enough, every time that new members are admitted, all old members must state that they will take on the
additional burden of doing all in their power to increase the
new members' faith, confirm their hope, and perfect them
in love! Perfect them in love, indeed!

Remember, all those vows are in addition to the promise
to live a Christian life in every *non*specified way possible.
It is no wonder that Christians get tired and tense. One
might suspect that they would turn out to be the tiredest and
tensest, the most compressed and anxious people on the
planet!

Doug Ross, the executive director of the Evangelical
Christian Publishers Association, wrote an article titled
" 'Relax' Is Not a Four-Letter Word." He said, "Maybe
you're uneasy with idleness. Maybe you never admit to
relaxing. In my opinion," he continued, "this pervades the
evangelical Christian community. If you read a book, it
should be a serious book. If you watch television, it had
better be the news, or possibly 'Sixty Minutes.' If you admit
to travel, it must be a business trip. And if you admit to a
vacation, it should be a 'working vacation.' "[1]

Ross confessed that he and his wife had recently learned
the joy of having a week of vacation with nothing to do. A
friend reacted dubiously to that possibility, saying that after
three days he wouldn't know what to do; but the Rosses
reported they had rediscovered the full meaning of Acts
3:19, which speaks of "times of refreshing" that shall come
from the Lord. Doug Ross concluded, "Surely those times

included prayer, Bible reading, church, and so forth. But does it stretch our theological imagination too far to believe it means that we need to stop our busy world and get off for some relaxation? I think not.''

The antidote to stress is rest: rest from duties, rest from frustration, rest from demands, rest from irritations, rest from tension, rest from schedules. Unfortunately, not only is our culture ''compressed,'' it is also loath to sanction rest and relaxation. We are victims of a double whammy— a hurry-worry life-style coupled with don't-take-off-from-work values. *Newsweek* author Robert J. Samuelson wrote about this in an article entitled ''Rediscovering the Rat Race.'' But reality as he sees it is a rude antithesis to Ross's call for more relaxation. Samuelson wrote, ''Our culture is uneasy with idleness. . . . Americans are reluctant to admit they spend too much time relaxing. Is it any wonder, then, that even the term 'leisure' is becoming dated. Media and marketing consultants now talk of 'discretionary time'—the idea being that, if you've made a choice about how to use your time, then it's no longer free and enjoyable.''[2]

This is a disturbing commentary on our culture. However, the situation is not hopeless, as the Rosses illustrated with their ability to enjoy a taskless vacation even when they did not think they would. What Samuelson's analysis does mean is that we who would learn how to relax must become countercultural. We will find little help in our workaday environment. Thus, we will have to work harder to become more relaxed. That sounds like a contradiction in terms, but what I mean is that we shall have to become serious about reading, hearing, and pondering over such messages as this one. We cannot take lightly our need to bring life back under some control. We shall have to become earnest in our efforts to desist from our overearnest ways of existing.

We must begin with ourselves. Coming right up is a questionnaire for you to take. Feel free to photocopy it if several of you are reading the book together. It is meant to enlighten you as to your basic approach to life.

The questionnaire is designed to help you assess the degree to which you are a Type A personality who assertively and tensely attacks life with impatience and high expectation of achievement. Do not be put off by the "Type A" label; we are all together in this venture. You will likely be the exception if you do not tend in some degree toward Type A. The questionnaire is intended to help you look at yourself. It has no other meaning. The higher the score, the more you are a Type A person.

Incidentally, even if you do not score strongly toward Type A, you may still be stress-filled, as you will see in the next chapter. There it will become obvious that life has a way of being frustrating to almost all of us.

However, you should be aware from the beginning that I am convinced that becoming a relaxed, peaceful person requires that we look at our spiritual as well as our daily lives. In fact, I'll be so bold as to say that the root of our problem may be spiritual. Not that we will not profit from analyzing our stresses and learning methods of relaxing ourselves. These will be valuable in and of themselves. But hypertension, stress, and strain are fundamentally a spiritual disorder, one grounded in a conflict over beliefs, values, and life goals. I agree with the theologian Donald Tubesing, who concluded, "People experiencing excessive stress need more than relaxation training. To deal with the source of their stress they need . . . assistance in examining their spiritual outlook. . . . They need to rethink their most basic assumptions about life and what makes it worthwhile."[3]

And now you know where I stand as we begin this journey together.

This questionnaire was designed by Archibald Hart, and with his permission is reprinted here from his book *The Hidden Link Between Adrenaline and Stress* (1986, Dallas, Texas: Word).

TYPE A BEHAVIOR PATTERN TEST

Read each question carefully and give yourself a rating according to the following descriptions:

Rating	Description
0	This statement does not apply to me.
1	It sometimes (less than once a month) applies to me.
2	It often (more than once a month) applies to me.

STATEMENT	RATING
1. I feel as if there isn't enough time in each day to do all the things I need to do.	( )
2. I tend to speak faster than most people, even finishing their sentences for them.	( )
3. My spouse or friends say, or I believe, that I eat too quickly.	( )
4. I tend to get very upset when I lose a game.	( )
5. I am very competitive in work, sports, or games.	( )
6. I tend to be bossy and dominate others.	( )
7. I prefer to lead rather than to follow.	( )
8. I feel pressed for time even when I am not doing something important.	( )

9. I become impatient when I have to wait.   ( )
10. I tend to make decisions quickly, even impulsively.   ( )
11. I regularly take on more than I can accomplish.   ( )
12. I become irritable (even angry) more often than most people.   ( )

TOTAL   _____

In the world you have much tribulation. . . .
—JESUS (JOHN 16:33)

CHAPTER 2

Stress and Strain in Daily Life

The catalogue of Occidental College, a liberal arts institution in southern California, used to state that the college was "nestled between picturesque Glendale and stately Pasadena." Not anymore. The 1991 catalogue proclaims that Occidental is "only twenty minutes from the downtown of vital, bustling Los Angeles." This complete change of viewpoint reflects the increased speed and pressure with which most of us live. In Occidental's neighborhood that difference is nowhere better exemplified than in contrasting Los Angeles's first freeway, just off the Occidental campus, to the monstrous arteries—five lanes each way—that take millions in and out of the metropolis each day. There are those straight-as-an-arrow gargantuan constructions; and then there is the weaving, curvaceous Pasadena freeway, built shortly after the turn of the century over ox-cart ruts.

The proximity to urbanity that the Occidental College catalogue pictures as an advantage is experienced by many others as a major source of stress. Although studies show that population density by itself is not an index of stress, one can't help but wonder if the growth that has caused even the largest freeways in Los Angeles to become "mobile parking lots" has not also meant a significant increase in the tension experienced by those who must spend hours of their time creeping to and from their jobs.

Today, most people who live or work in cities do exist under significant stress and strain. I suspect, however, that the major causes of stress are more personal than cultural, more internal than environmental. In chapter 1 we looked at some of the stresses that plague individuals; in this chapter we'll classify those stresses around some basic themes. Putting names to problems is usually helpful in solving them. The list is not exhaustive, but it does highlight many of the major issues we all must deal with. Do not hesitate to add to the list from your own experience.

STRESS: A DEFINITION

Before we go further, let's try to establish a definition of stress. Hans Selye, the foremost authority on the subject, states in his well-known book *The Stress of Life* that stress is "the nonspecific response to any demand, including efforts to cope with the *wear and tear* in the body caused by life at any one time."[1] Selye adds that stress is a common feature of all biologic activity at any time.

We can break Selye's definition down into simpler words: He is saying that stress is what occurs when people do anything, anytime, anywhere. Getting up off the chair and walking over to change the television station involves stress, according to Selye. Of course, nowadays we don't have to rise from our chair. We punch a button on a remote control device and—presto!—station changes can be accomplished at an astounding rate. According to my wife, there is much more stress in watching my "flipping" of television channels than there is in the act of changing stations. Yet even in the pressing of a button there is the exertion of energy; and that button pressing is stress, according to Selye.

I suppose the only time people may not be under stress is when they have gone to sleep—perhaps even while looking at the television (a behavior I am often accused of). Yet, if one dreamed during these TV naps, I guess that dreaming, too, would take a certain amount of energy and be called "stress." (And if the dream is a nightmare . . .)

As you can see, Selye did not define the term in the way we commonly think of it. Most of us would probably have defined stress as something different from simply using our energy any old which way.

EUSTRESS AND DISTRESS

Selye actually does make a distinction that comes closer to what we might normally think of when we use the word *stress*. He contrasts "good" stress with "bad." He states, "We must . . . differentiate within the general concept of stress between the unpleasant or harmful variety, called *distress* (from the Latin *dis* = bad, as in dissonance, disagreement), and *eustress* (from the Greek *ed* = good, as in euphonia, euphoria)."[2] According to Selye, our bodies react the same way to both. What makes the difference is how we take the experience, not whether the action itself is in response to a positive or a negative stimulus. For example, practically no one would describe getting caught in a traffic jam on a Los Angeles freeway at five in the afternoon as a pleasant experience. It is a negative event.

Yet Selye would say that if one relaxes and uses the time to talk with fellow passengers or, if one is alone, to listen to tapes or the radio, even the experience of being caught in a traffic jam can be eustress rather than distress.

On the other hand, what might appear to be a positive event can turn out to be distressful, as the old television program "The Millionaire" illustrated. Here people were singled out for receiving a million dollars from an unknown benefactor. The near tragedies that such a gift sometimes provoked were clearly distressful. I have few friends, however, who would not let such examples of distress hold them back from saying, "Bring on the money; I'll take my chances!" In a less dramatic way, getting married, being promoted, winning a scholarship, graduating from college, and taking a vacation are all pleasant events that nevertheless have the potential for becoming distressful.

Selye makes a good point in distinguishing between eustress and distress. As we consider the several types of stress that people encounter, we will see whether his conviction that all negative experiences can be turned into good stress holds up. My conviction is that, to a great degree, it does.

SUCCESS, STRESS, AND DISTRESS

Building on Selye's distinction between good and bad stress, I have designed a threefold model for looking at the issue. Instead of a twofold distinction, my model uses three terms to describe the types of feelings we have whenever we expend our energies in action. I believe it solves the problem of thinking of every human action as involving "stress."

The three terms of my model are Success, Stress, and Distress.

SUCCESS We experience "success" when we meet a challenge, solve a problem, accomplish a task, win a race, convince a friend, or receive a compliment,—to mention only a few experiences of success. What they have in common is that when we exert ourselves, we reach our goals. We get what we want. And what we want in life is affection, appreciation, and affirmation. Although it is true that in reaching our goals we expended some energy and maybe even made some sacrifices, we would not dare to think of our successful activities as "stressful" events.

Two examples of success that I admire are when a radio announcer calls a basketball game well and when a square dance caller leads a dance in a sprightly fashion. I feel sure that both the radio announcer and the square dance caller would say, "Boy, was that exciting. I really got worked up—but I made it." They would not define the experience as stress-filled.

STRESS We experience "stress" when we don't meet the challenge as well as we hoped; when we experience resistance, have to take a detour, don't get hired for a job, lose some money, can't meet deadlines, fail to do our duty, make mistakes in a recital, forget to pay a bill, are notified our rent is raised, or don't get what we want. What ties together all such situations is our having to overcome major obstacles to reach our goals. Sometimes we are successful in overcoming them, and sometimes we are not. In every case, when it's over, we know we've "been through the wringer." We have put out a lot of extra energy we had not planned on using, or had hoped we'd not have to use, and we know it. We feel stressed.

Two examples of stress from my own life are my failure to get accepted to graduate school the first time I applied and my father's death when I was six years old. Neither event was in my plans, to say the least. As you read them, remember that I describe them as "stress"—not "distress." Although they were very troubling, they did not overwhelm me.

On one early spring Saturday in March 1937, my cousins and I were sent to the neighborhood movie theater. My father had been ill. I came back from a movie expecting my father to be up from his sickbed, only to be told by my mother, "Daddy has gone to be with God, and we must so live that we will be able to join him someday." She added that God would send his guardian angel to take care of us. However, her words did not take away the shock, dismay, and confusion I was feeling. I was filled with stress.

Some twenty-three years later, I headed home to Decatur, Alabama, from Nashville, Tennessee, the site of Vanderbilt University, full of plans to move my family there. At Vanderbilt, I thought, I would surely be admitted to graduate study in psychology. I had taken the Miller's Analogies Test at the university and been told that if my score was high enough, I would be admitted. I had never failed anything in my life, so of course I anticipated that I would knock the top off that test. I settled my family in a new house and went over on the first day of class. I said to the secretary, "I'm ready to start classes for my doctorate," only to be told, "We did not admit you; you only passed the Miller's Analogies Test at the fifty-fifth percentile." That was not what I wanted to hear.

Those were stress-filled experiences for a six-year-old and a twenty-nine-year-old! However, I survived them both. I remember crying every night after my father's death; then every other night; then every week, month, and year. Now, I weep only when I visit his grave. Although I still miss him, I have managed life without him. The stress subsided, and I have survived. The twenty-nine-year-old pleaded successfully with nearby Peabody College: Try me as a special student, I said, until I prove myself able to do graduate work in psychology. I turned a near disaster into a possibility. Several years later I graduated and could say to the Vanderbilt psychology department, "You missed a good thing!"

St. Paul illustrated this distinction between stress and distress in his second letter to the Corinthians. He wrote: "We are afflicted in every way, but not crushed; perplexed, but not driven to despair; persecuted, but not forsaken; struck down, but not destroyed. . . ." (4:8).

DISTRESS Distress is another matter. Distress is more than "a lot of stress that we survive or that we turn into success later on." Distress is our lot when we fail to overcome obstacles and lose our self-confidence to boot.

The difference between stress and distress is how threatened we feel. There can be much stress with little distress. The reverse is true. There can be little outer stress and much distress. It is possible to experience distress when we lose an election, don't get a promotion, have an argument with our spouse, fail a test, overdraw our checking account, hear our child has been arrested, have our car's motor break down, or are fired from a job—to mention only a few experiences that can become distressful. However, distress is not automatic. If our opinion of ourselves is deeply shaken, we may move over the line from stress to distress.

A client came to me for counseling after her fiancé committed suicide. She was devastated. She and her fiancé had set the date for their wedding. Although she knew that he was having a difficult time in his business, she thought that their love was sufficient to carry him through those problems. It had surprised and shocked her when she had phoned him for two days and he had not answered. She went over to see him and found him dead on the floor from a drug overdose. She called me, distraught and fearful that she would take her own life. She felt that her whole life was ruined. She did not know what to do with herself. Her self-confidence disappeared.

The president of American University, who had been apprehended for making obscene phone calls, said in a newspaper interview that being caught in his deviant behavior and having to resign his presidency constituted the most embarrassing moment in his life. Further, his wife had not known that he had become entwined in a sexual obsession and had been using his official phone to make obscene phone calls to numbers taken at random from the phone book. He felt compelled to make those calls on certain days and at certain times. As the months passed, he found himself more excited by the calls and by their increasing news coverage and became less discreet in making them. Finally his calls were traced and he was caught. He had seemed oblivious of the risk of his behavior; now he became aware of the enormity of his transgression and said that the discovery was the worst day of his life. He lost his self-esteem. In both those examples, stress became distress.

Remember that I began this discussion with a list of events that I suggested we *can* experience as distressful. I did not say we automatically *do*. There is nothing inevitable about distress. Events such as I mentioned are highly stressful, to be sure. In many situations, we put out a lot of energy and still the worst happens. However, the line between stress and distress need not be crossed unless we lose our self-esteem. Obviously our self-esteem is threatened or undermined when we are stressed. But threat and loss are two different things. The term distress should be applied only

Figure 1.   A Comparison of Malony and Selye Models

Eustress (*good*)		Distress (*bad*)
	Selye	

Success	Stress	Distress
	Malony	

when we altogether *lose* our self-esteem and find ourselves putting enormous additional energy into trying to get it back or agonizing over our loss in a way that paralyzes recuperative action.

The preceding figure shows how Selye's model and mine can be related. As you can see, my model goes beyond his at both ends. Much of what he would think of as "good stress" (eustress) I call "success." I also extend his understanding of "distress" by dividing it into surmountable/survivable "stress" and devastating/debilitating "distress," in which people lose their self-confidence and self-esteem. I think that most of our time is spent in the "stress" area, somewhat less time is spent in the "success" area, and almost all of us go into the "distress" area from time to time.

To a degree, the old maxim is true: It's not so much what happens to you, it's how you take what happens. I say "to a degree" because most of us believe that certain events would be deeply devastating to anybody. The death of someone you deeply love, such as a husband or wife, would be an example. Yet, even here, some folk are not overwhelmed; they do not lose their self-esteem when death occurs. I heard a comedienne do a monologue on a woman whose husband had just died. She declared he was a "no-good, freeloading, worthless skunk." A bystander exclaimed, "Surely you can

say something good about the dead." "I sure can, honey,"
the widow replied. "He's dead. That's good!"

In a more serious vein, *Psychology Today* reported research on widows and widowers that suggested that women
whose husbands died after a long-term illness were more
likely to die themselves soon thereafter than women whose
husbands died suddenly. The reverse was true for men. Men
whose wives die suddenly are not prepared to take care of
themselves, but those men whose wives die after being sick
a long time have learned to care for themselves. However,
women who have had to attend to husbands with chronic
illnesses are much more likely to be physically and finan-
cially exhausted after they lose their husbands. Women
whose husbands die suddenly are much better prepared to
care for themselves. These facts show how much personal
interpretations and life situations can enter into how one
reacts to disaster. On the surface, it would seem that people
could handle better those stressful events that they know
are coming, and thus can prepare for, than those that happen
suddenly. But that is not always true.

I know I am spending a lot of space talking about stress
experiences. You are probably itching for me to get down
to describing some of them. And I will do so soon. Yet, I
think it's important for us to have some framework in which
to place our descriptions. The models I have been describing
are one type of helpful structure. This research on how men
and women react to the death of a spouse adds another plank
to our understanding. It shows us how having or not having
personal inner resources when the stress comes makes all
the difference in how we handle it; in other words, whether
we go from stress to distress.

NOW AND THEN, ONE OR MANY, IN AND OUT, MORE OR LESS

It goes without saying that sometimes we become distressed over an experience that at another time would probably occasion only stress. I call this the "Now and Then" principle. It all depends on whether we have the resources to manage the situation and whether our self-esteem is threatened or not—at the time. If we are under several other pressures, we will be more likely to become distressed than if what happened was the only thing we had to deal with. I call this the "One or Many" principle.

There are two variations on this theme. As we experience pressure over some event, we sometimes find ourselves feeling "distressed" at one minute and only "stressed" at another. Our self-esteem seems to be lost and then found—both in a short period of time. This can happen again and again as, for example, when we have an argument with someone we love. I call this the "In and Out" principle. Finally there is the "More or Less" principle; that means we can be just a little distressed or greatly distressed depending on whether we feel our self-esteem is slightly or deeply threatened. For example, we all know the difference between having a certain behavior gently criticized and being devastated and embarrassed by someone who does not like us.

ACCIDENTS, BREAKDOWNS, AND CHANGES

Now to describe the types of experiences that are stressful for so many of us so much of the time. I group them under three headings: Accidents, Breakdowns, and Changes. Accidents are those events we did not expect. Breakdowns are those problems that arise when things do not go as we had planned. Changes are those stressful experiences we will have if we live long enough and the life cycle and human nature function as, more or less, they always have. Accidents are the things we never thought would happen; breakdowns are those things we hoped would not occur; and changes are those things that are destined to occur over time.

Accidents usually are tragic losses of one kind or another. The experience of a house burning down, an automobile wreck, a divorce, the loss of a job, an assault, a robbery, a sudden death, a potentially terminal illness, a deformed birth, the breakup of a friendship, consequences of an extramarital affair, the mental breakdown of a loved one—all are examples of the types of events that folk never expect to happen to them. As one parent on the video *When the Music Stops* said about a daughter who had become schizophrenic at age fifteen: "We never thought in a million years this would happen to us. Our daughter was an accomplished pianist. We knew we were in for trouble the night we heard her downstairs trying, but being unable, to play simple scales." No amount of planning or anticipation could prepare this family for the stress they experienced when their daughter became ill. Accidents provoke stress in everyone they touch. Often lives are so radically changed that the tension aroused seems never to subside. Families who have had loved ones killed by drunk drivers are vivid examples of this type of stress.

Breakdowns usually involve plans gone amiss. They may involve the like of unexpected sickness; automobile malfunctions; plant shutdowns; major house repairs; emergency expenditures; moving to different neighborhoods; changes in other people's feelings, ambitions, and expectations. In every breakdown we know beforehand that something *could* go wrong but we hope it won't. Breakdowns are the essence of Murphy's Law: "If something can go wrong, it will."

In contrast to accidents, breakdowns can be anticipated; often, in some degree, they are even expected. We hope breakdowns will not occur, but we know that, at any time, they may. As one friend said to me, "We were trying to make our older car last one more year, but we knew the transmission might break down, and it did!" Another friend, who was getting a divorce, confessed, "I guess I thought she was a different person; she turned out to be more cautious and less venturesome than I ever imagined. It's sad," he continued, "but we are just not compatible." Yet another friend reported, "We knew our son would have some adjustment problems when we moved from Miami to Chicago, but we hoped his grades would hold up; it's been a hard first year." These are examples of breakdowns. Stress and strain are inevitable when breakdowns happen, no matter to what extent we expect them.

Changes are the inevitable events (both good and bad) that occur in our lives if we live long enough. Babies become children; children become adolescents; adolescents become young adults; young adults become adults; adults grow old; old people die. When we are young, time drags; we think in terms of months and half years. We say, "I'm almost five," or "I'm four and a half." When we are adolescent we are often described as "sixteen going on twenty-five." When we are at mid-life time rushes by, and we state, "I'm only fifty-five." Toward the end of life, time drags and then stands still. As Shakespeare wrote, "All the world's a stage, and all the men and women merely players: They have their exits and their entrances." Time pushes us along into new roles, and our realization of how different life seems at various times can be extremely stressful. Change comes to all of us, and the stress that goes with those changes can be fully predicted but never pre-experienced—as any mother will confess after the delivery of her first baby.

Having to find a job, attending your first child's marriage, experiencing one's first chronic illness, retiring from a job, no longer being able to drive a car, dying—all are changes that include stress. In fact, our *knowing* that certain events are in the future may provoke more worry and strain than the changes themselves. I have a friend who is so preoccupied with earthquakes in southern California that she keeps her radio on over eighteen hours each day. She wants to be the first to know when the inevitable occurs—even if the earthquake is so far away she could not possibly feel it. She worries herself sick and is the butt of many an office joke! Yes, changes are planned for, worried about, and, finally, experienced. Change-related stress in our lives is the rule, not the exception.

"SELF" PROTECTION

Earlier I said that whether an event was experienced as stressful or not depended on one's personal situation at the time of the event. Remember the principles of In and Out, Now and Then, More or Less, and One or Many? Well, the one thing that underlies all of those features of specific events is our deep need to protect our self-esteem from attack. When we achieve our goals or overcome resistance, we feel self-affirmed and victorious. When we are outwitted or overpowered, we experience defeat and anxiety. Our security is shaken. When that happens, as we have seen, our stress can become distress. And (as we will describe in more detail a bit further on) when stress becomes distress, our bodies react by getting us prepared for a fight. Animating our red-alert brains, our tense muscles, our keen eyesight, and our enraged emotions is the need to maintain our self-esteem.

Our need to achieve our goals, to perform well, to earn more money, to be given higher positions, to win more awards, to sustain our friendships, to find someone to love, to be complimented and recognized, to avoid losses, to evade loneliness, to safeguard our riches, to demonstrate our courage, to pursue our dreams—all those needs and more are grounded in a compulsion to establish and maintain our self-esteem. We must not forget that the very core of stress is our uncertainty about the answer to one question: Will I be able to handle this situation wisely, effectively, gracefully?

Among the signs of the kind of stress that borders on distress are the following. How many of them are you experiencing? Put a check by each one that has happened to you in the last month.

- inability to slow down (   )

- mind racing so that sleep was difficult (   )

- inability to concentrate (   )

- fatigued but couldn't get to sleep (   )

- feelings of worthlessness or hopelessness (   )

- nervousness, trembling, dizziness (   )

- worried, uptight feeling (   )

- vague fears that something bad was about to happen (   )

But remember, underneath any or all of these symptoms is the problem of self-esteem. It may well be true that most of us suffer from the *imposter syndrome*, about which much has been written. This is the constant feeling that we are about to be exposed. Our security is always at risk, so much of the time we are under stress. We feel under attack; frequently we feel we must defend ourselves. Our self-esteem may be only skin-deep. Our persistent fear is that our real self will be disclosed and that all our achievements and acquisitions will be taken away from us. Then our inner inadequacy will be revealed like a spoiled banana underneath an unblemished skin. These are our real concerns underneath our stress.

The following checklist will help you assess the amount of stress you might be experiencing. The checklist includes both positive and negative events and asks you to indicate how recently these events occurred. It assumes that if a situation happened long ago, you may have adjusted to it by now. However, as you complete the list—do not be discouraged. There is hope, as we shall see in the chapter to come.

LIFE EVENT CHECKLIST[3]

Life Events	Within past year	1–5 years ago	Over 5 years ago
1. death of spouse..............	( )	( )	( )
2. institutionalization (for example: nursing home, psychiatric hospital, prison).....	( )	( )	( )
3. death of a close family member	( )	( )	( )

Life Events	Within past year	1–5 years ago	Over 5 years ago
4. major personal injury (for example: auto accident or fall that is still a problem)...	( )	( )	( )
5. major personal illness that is still a problem...............	( )	( )	( )
6. getting a divorce	( )	( )	( )
7. being fired from work	( )	( )	( )
8. major personal injury that is no longer a problem.........	( )	( )	( )
9. major personal illness that is no longer a problem.........	( )	( )	( )
10. major change in financial state	( )	( )	( )
11. retirement	( )	( )	( )
12. marital separation	( )	( )	( )
13. being physically or sexually abused.......................	( )	( )	( )
14. getting married	( )	( )	( )
15. death of a close friend.......	( )	( )	( )
16. major change to a family member or relative (including health, finances, relationships)	( )	( )	( )
17. major change in gratifying activities....................	( )	( )	( )
18. major change in sexual behavior.....................	( )	( )	( )
19. major change in work responsibilities	( )	( )	( )
20. change in residence	( )	( )	( )
21. change to a different line of work	( )	( )	( )
22. pregnancy	( )	( )	( )
23. spouse's starting or stopping work	( )	( )	( )

Life Events	Within past year	1–5 years ago	Over 5 years ago
24. major change in living conditions or environment	( )	( )	( )
25. marital reconciliation	( )	( )	( )
26. major business readjustment (bankruptcy, relocation, merger).....................	( )	( )	( )
27. major change in social activities.....................	( )	( )	( )
28. major increase in family arguments	( )	( )	( )
29. losing driver's license	( )	( )	( )
30. major change in number of people living in the home ...	( )	( )	( )
31. reaching sixty-five years of age	( )	( )	( )
32. reaching seventy years of age	( )	( )	( )
33. major in-law troubles........	( )	( )	( )
34. major change in working hours or conditions..........	( )	( )	( )
35. major troubles with the boss	( )	( )	( )
36. holidays, anniversaries spent alone	( )	( )	( )
37. outstanding personal achievement	( )	( )	( )
38. major revision of personal habits	( )	( )	( )

Please check any of these events that occured during your childhood or adolescence:

39. unwed pregnancy	( )
40. divorce of parents	( )
41. marital separation of parents	( )

Life Events	Within past year	1–5 years ago	Over 5 years ago
42. having a visible physical deformity			( )
43. being involved with alcohol or drugs			( )
44. jail sentence of a parent			( )
45. discovery of being adopted			( )
46. major change in acceptance by childhood peers			( )
47. marriage of parent to a stepparent			( )
48. pregnancy of an unwed teenage sister			( )
49. failure to be passed to the next grade in school			( )
50. frequent changes to new schools			( )

NOTES

A scoring key for the checklist is on pages 147-148. It shows how much *stress* you are presently under. It does not tell you how much *distress* you are experiencing. Only you can say. However, it is reasonable to presume that if you are under a great amount of stress, there is the likelihood that you will be very near to distress. In Atkinson's study an average score of 447 was found. Scores could possibly go as high as 1897 for an older person.

1. Selye p. 398
2. Selye p. 74
3. Atkinson, B. E. (1986). Religious Maturity and Psychological Distress Among Older Christian Women. (Ph.D. Dissertation, Fuller Theological Seminary)

If you can keep your head while those about you
are losing theirs and blaming it upon you . . .
then you will be a man, my son.
—RUDYARD KIPLING, "IF"

CHAPTER 3

Like Yourself:
The Secret of Relaxation

Sentries feel threatened. They are always tense, always on guard. The fear we feel when a dog growls or snarls at us goes away when we've run to safety or seen that the animal is behind a fence; but a sentry, who puts a brave face on fear, has to remain on guard. The enemy may be somewhere out there in the dark and could attack at any time. Who knows when or from where the assault will come?

Sentries must remain on guard until other sentries relieve them of their posts. Their very existence is threatened if they relax their vigilance; they *must* remain hypertense. Sentries sometimes have a problem calming down even when they are off duty. They jolt awake from sleep, afraid they have been caught "off guard."

Life can be like that. We can live life as if we are sentries. Most of the time, however, the threat we feel is less to our physical bodies and more to our psychological selves. Who of us would not admit that our self-concepts, our reputations, our feelings about ourselves are extremely important? If we are embarrassed, or challenged, or accused, or doubted, or disliked, we will become as tense as if we were sentries defending a gate. When we are given a speeding ticket by a policeman or receive a failing grade on a test; when our dog soils a neighbor's patio; when we fail to meet a sales goal; when we have an argument with someone we love; when we lose a game; when we are criticized for our opinions; when we are compared to someone who used to "do it better"; when we forget a promise—all of these are threats to our self-esteem. And if we lose our self-respect, if we feel we've received too many threats to our self-esteem, we can become just as hypertense as any sentry guarding any fortress around the world.

Yes, that's what stress is: a threat to our self-esteem. Stress is a threat to our reputation, what others think about us, as well as our status, the role we play in life. For example, if Veronica hears someone say, "Veronica is a gossip, she can't keep a secret; don't tell her anything you don't want the whole world to know," she will feel threatened because her reputation is being questioned. However, if Veronica gets fired from her job at Burger King, she will feel threatened because her status has been lowered.

The self-esteem formula looks like this: R (reputation) plus S (status) = SE (self-esteem). We are fragile individuals. All of us have experienced the "Veronica syndrome" to one degree or another. Only when our reputation and our status together add up to a positive sum is our self-esteem strong enough for us to be anywhere near stress-free. And we all know how easy it is for that sum to be negative. That's when we feel stressed and need to learn how to relax.

We cannot relax when we feel threatened. We automatically put up our guard to protect our reputation and our status. We want to have a role to play in life, and we want to be liked and loved. When threat comes, we want to get rid of it and regain our self-esteem. We want things to settle down and return to normal. And normal means when we feel good about ourselves.

Actually life is lived under three conditions: Success, Stress, and Distress. Success is the condition we all like and yearn for. It's the normal situation. Here we are successful in liking ourselves and in being liked by others. We feel safe and secure. Things go well for us. We have a role to play; a place in the world. We are recognized and respected. We like it.

I have an actress friend. You would probably recognize her if you saw her. Often she can be seen on TV playing the role of a middle-aged woman in sitcoms, advertisements, and specials. I can always recognize when she is living under the "success" umbrella. She is animated, cheerful, bold, assertive, and opinionated. She likes herself and moves through life in a relaxed, self-confident manner.

Sometimes, however, she experiences stress, the second of life's conditions. She auditions for parts she does not get. She goes through weeks in which she is not acting. She sits by the phone endless hours waiting for her agent to call. The pilot programs in which she has played a role are not bought by the networks. She experiences stress, and I can tell it when I am around her. She has a frown on her face; she looks worried. She walks with an awkward, overcontrolled gait. She ceases to laugh and share jokes with me. She speaks only when spoken to. Her self-esteem is under attack. Usually my actress friend's mood changes as a result of a phone call from her agent telling of a new opportunity. Typically her feelings alternate between elation and discouragement, depending on whether she is experiencing success or stress in her chosen vocation.

But sometimes things turn from bad to worse. Occasionally a whole season from November to May will pass without my friend's being offered a major acting role. She goes from stress to distress. She calls me every other day. She doubts herself. She feels worthless. She asks me to reassure her that she can act and that things will change. She finds it difficult to sleep at night. She feels exhausted much of the time, and her muscles ache. Those are all symptoms that she feels she is under constant threat. She is experiencing no relief. Her self-esteem is as low as it can get. She is no longer just stressed; she has become distressed.

When our reputation or our status is threatened, when the threat lasts too long and is too devastating, stress can indeed turn to distress.

On the other hand, relaxation and better self-esteem go together. Which comes first is hard to say. As the saying goes, "Flip a coin and take your choice." If you like yourself, you can relax; if you relax, you will like yourself. Whatever the answer, I am convinced that relaxing can calm us down enough so that regaining our self-esteem becomes a possibility—even when we are in great danger and facing a monumental threat. Like a ball of snow rolling down a mountain, relaxation can start a process that will gain momentum and result in our regaining self-confidence and self-affirmation. And this is possible, in my opinion, regardless of whether our reputation is always good in the sight of others or whether we hold positions that bring us power and money.

Take a moment before going to the next chapter. Put the book down and see if what I have described does not ring true for you. First, think of a time when you felt everything was good for you, when "all systems were go," when you were experiencing "success." Was it not true for you that you felt considerable self-esteem? (Here put the book down until you have a "success" time in mind.)

Was it not true that you liked the position you held and that your reputation was good? Well, maybe things weren't perfect, but didn't the sum of your reputation and your position add up to positive feelings about yourself?

After you have remembered a success experience, turn your attention to remembering a "stress" time in your life. Shut your eyes and recall it. See if you can reexperience the feelings you had at that time. (Here put the book down until you have a "stress" time in mind.)

Analyze what was going on. Was it not true that the real issue was a threat to your self-esteem? See if you can work the R + S = SE formula. Where was the danger? Was it to your reputation? Or your status? Where was the imbalance that added up to negative feelings about yourself? What happened to change the situation from stress back toward success? Or, what kept the situation from getting worse? How did you manage this stress experience?

Finally, before turning to the next chapter, recall a "distress" experience in your life. Even though you have probably wanted to forget it, be brave. Reexperience it in all its fury and tumult. Be sober. Don't get overwhelmed. Let the feelings come. (Here put the book down until you have a "distress" time in mind.)

Stand above it and analyze. See if what I have said was not true. You were devastated in your self-esteem and felt you had to fight for your life. At the time you had a sense that only the worst would follow. Again, work the R + S = SE formula. Put words to where the threat was frightening you. Was it not true that the distress made you tense all over? Ready to fight? Afraid of being annihilated? Hopeless?

A postscript: Thank goodness this chapter is not the last. Else you would feel I left you dangling with no way out. Remember, however, the note of encouragement I sounded. Stress can be handled if you learn how to relax. Read on. There is a way, and we will find it.

Those who have a "why" to live
can live through any "how."
—FRIEDRICH NIETZSCHE

Be still and know that I am God.
—PSALM 46:10

CHAPTER 4

Christian Reasons to Relax

Relaxation is a gift. We don't have to work for it or pay good money to get it. It's free! God gives it to us. As Jesus stated, "It is the Father's good pleasure to give you the kingdom" (Luke 12:32). Elsewhere we read that the "kingdom" is "abundant life" here and now (see Luke 12:22–31 and John 10:10). And being relaxed is part of abundant living. Living the relaxed life is one of God's intentions for us. Being relaxed is what the Bible means when it suggests we are to live "peaceably with all people" (Romans 12:18). Peace is one of the fruits of the Holy Spirit mentioned in Galatians (5:22), and Paul notes in 1 Corinthians that God "has called us to peace" (7:15). It pains and disappoints God when we are filled with stress and strain. So he gives relaxation to us, free for the asking. And relaxation is both the road to and the result of "the peace of God that passes all understanding" (Philippians 4:7).

Why? For what reason? What does being relaxed do for

us that pleases God? What on earth does relaxation accomplish that is part of God's kingdom? Why does God give us relaxation?

DO NO HARM The first reason is a simple one: to prevent us from harming one another. Sounds logical, doesn't it? When people are tired and stress-filled, they tend to make mistakes. We've all read headlines like "Truck driver falls asleep after driving fourteen hours; crash involves six vehicles—three dead." Does it need to be said that God does not approve of such accidents? The Bible states, "He remembers our frame, that we are dust" (Psalm 103:14). God knows we get tired and have a tendency toward stress. He intends for us to take care of ourselves; to stay relaxed lest we harm ourselves or others. Hippocrates made his first rule for physicians "Do no harm." Jesus said it would be better that people had millstones hung around their necks than that they harm one of the little ones brought to him (Luke 17:2).

God loves people. When we are tense, we run the risk of hurting each other. That is not God's wish. He intends that we be rested and relaxed when we deal with others. At the very least, we, like physicians, should do no harm. There is almost a one-to-one relationship between our stress and the likelihood that we will hurt others, accidentally or otherwise. What do people do when they lose their self-esteem or self-worth? They fight. And they do not care whom they hurt. Jesus calls for us to refrain from anger with each other and to love even our enemies (Matthew 5:21–26 and 5:43–48). Not getting angry, much less loving others, is difficult under the best of conditions. When we are stressed or distressed, we will find these almost impossible.

DO YOUR BEST Being able to do one's best is a second reason God would have us learn to relax. The "home-court advantage'' is a factor well known to basketball players and their coaches. Traveling long distances the day before the game and sleeping in a strange bed are trying experiences that make winning doubly hard. To perform well consistently, we all need to have the ''home-court advantage'' in life; to be relaxed when we get out on the playing field. This is the will of God.

St. Paul compares Christian living to another type of athletic encounter. Run life's good race, he recommends to us, in ''such a way that you might win it'' (1 Corinthians 9:24b). He suggests that toward that end we are to put on such shoes as will make us ''ready to proclaim the gospel of peace'' (Ephesians 6:15). We can find no better running shoes than those available under the ''relaxation'' brand. To run relaxed means to be at peace. Being relaxed makes it possible, in the words of the writer of Hebrews, ''to run with perseverance the race that is set before us'' (12:1b).

TEMPLE OF THE HOLY SPIRIT The Bible states that the body is the temple of the Holy Spirit (1 Corinthians 6:19). The body houses the race runner. Our status as spiritual beings requires that our bodies be in good shape. The body is like an automobile. Automobiles do not make decisions about where they shall go; people make those decisions. The body, like an automobile, is at the disposal of the person who inhabits it. God's intention is that our spirits function in healthy bodies.

Relaxing is like greasing the automobile. God did not separate the spirit from the body as we separate the driver from the automobile. Nor should we. God will be disappointed if hypertension is the cause of any mistake we make or anytime we fail in this life. There is no more important reason for Christians to relax than to keep the body a fit place for Christ to dwell within us.

THE EXAMPLE OF CHRIST Yet another reason for Christians to relax is to be found in the teaching and example of Christ. He encouraged us to "Be not anxious—but to seek first God's kingdom" (Matthew 5:25ff). He taught this truth. He lived it. No one could accuse Jesus of being anxious. He was calmness personified. Angered he might be on occasion, but anxious he was not. Homeless he roamed, but anxious he was not. Scared he became, but anxious he was not. What Christ did in the Garden of Gethsemane was to pray and relax himself. He practiced what he preached. When there was the chance that he would become distressed, he prayed. He kept God's will foremost in his mind. "Not my will but thine be done," he said (Matthew 26:39b). So should we. There is no doubt about his will for us. We are to follow him and learn to keep ourselves relaxed, even in the most threatening of circumstances.

There is an old gospel hymn that goes like this:

> Keep your eyes upon Jesus,
> look full in his wonderful face,
> And the things of earth will grow strangely dim,
> In the light of his glory and grace.

And these "things of earth" will, indeed, pale in importance if we just calm down and relax. That is God's will. That was his example. We should do likewise if we want to please him.

CHRIST TO OUR NEIGHBORS God wants us to be Christ to our neighbors. We do this by being good examples of what the good news can do with our lives. We do this by acting in loving ways. Unfortunately far too many Christians are workaholic examples. They are tense, tight, traumatizing folk who offend others with their strained behavior. No one wants to be like them. Whatever attraction to the Christian life might come from their example is lost. They're not good examples; they're bad news.

There is no substitute for the "real thing," as Coca-Cola ads remind us. That's as true as tomorrow's sunrise. Moreover, stressed-out folk are poor lovers. Too often married couples will attest to that. "I'm tired tonight" is the swan song of love unfulfilled. What's true of marriage is true in life. Stress-filled, tired Christians do not good lovers make! God wants us to love one another. In fact, Jesus said that our loving one another was the mark by which people would know that we were his disciples (John 13:35). We love best when we are calm, cool, and collected; in other words "relaxed." The touch of love should be gentle and lingering, not rough and hurried. This is the will of God. This is the way we become Christ to our neighbors.

So if anyone asks, "Why should Christians relax?" what will you say? How will you answer them? I have given some answers—but they are not the only ones. Take time before going on to the next chapter and consider again my five reasons, listed below, for Christians to relax. Ask yourself, "Do I agree?" What reason, or reasons, would you add? Lengthen this list accordingly.

• To keep us from harming ourselves and others

• To make it possible for us to do our best

- To provide a fit temple for the Holy Spirit
- To follow the example of Jesus
- To be Christ to our neighbor

There is more to life than speed.
—GANDHI

Vision is the art of seeing things invisible.
—JONATHAN SWIFT

CHAPTER 5

What Does It Mean to Relax?

Before we talk about how to relax, we need to better understand what it means to relax. The mistake we most commonly make is thinking that relaxing is synonymous with sleeping or with some state of dulled awareness.

How often have we heard someone say, "All I need is some sleep"? Yet how often have we heard those same people say, "I got up tired even though I slept for eight hours"? They don't realize that relaxing and sleeping are two different things.

Relaxing is something we do while we are wide awake.

Even more to the point, relaxation is a skill to be acquired and used while we are still at work. I am convinced that those who think of relaxation as something that is best done off the firing line of life miss the point. Real relaxation skills are those that can be practiced in the midst of the stress of life.

I once read a letter, written by Eugene Mainelli of Oakland, California, that underscores my conviction about where relaxation can best be found, especially for Christians. In his letter, written to the editor of the newsletter of his Roman Catholic diocese, Mainelli protested against his church's tendency to think that people had to get away on retreats to find themselves. He stated, "When we face the questions of life and death, bills and taxes, civic and neighborhood responsibilities, we need people on the streets to guide our search for the Christian way. . . . We don't have time for weekend retreats. Besides, what is there to retreat from? Sunday to Sunday, work and play, alone and together, we are living the Christian life to which we were called in baptism and the sacrament of matrimony." Better, according to Mainelli, that the leaders of the church spend their energies "listening, discovering, sharing in the giftedness that already is present in the believing community."

Agreeing with Mainelli, I intend to define relaxation as something quite distinct from sleep and as a skill to be utilized within daily tasks designed to make life more peaceful and more pleasing to God. I believe that being relaxed can be understood as reflecting, renewing, resting, recreating, regaining, restoring, and reinstating—the "seven Rs" of relaxation. Let me illustrate them one by one. Hopefully they will suggest the results we anticipate when we learn to relax. You will note that they are expressed as active participles rather than nouns. Relaxing is an active, living process, not a static state.

REFLECTING Relaxing means reflecting; learning how to think about stress and strain in a new way. When we reflect, we stand apart from a situation and gain perspective on it; we see it in a new light.

I looked out the window of my seventeenth-floor hotel room in Dearborn, Michigan, during a visit to that city and scanned the landscape. It looked like freeways and farm-lands to me. Later on I was told that nestled in the view was the Ford museum. I had wanted to go there but didn't realize it was so close. I looked out that same window and saw the museum clearly. Reflection helped me see that things are not always as they appear. Relaxing means re-flecting—stepping back a bit from whatever is upsetting us and gaining a new point of view; looking for some new vision. Reflecting is like putting on new prescription eye-glasses. We now see what we were previously blind to.

RENEWING Relaxing is renewing. Renewing means to rejuvenate our will to try again. Like muscles in which the lactic acid builds up, fatiguing them, maybe giving us a charley horse, our minds become tired when we experience frustration and failure. By learning to relax we find the strength to return to our problems and make a new effort to solve them. The tendency to throw up our hands and give up is overcome.

There is no running water at my mountain cabin. I have to fill huge containers at a spring over two hundred yards away. On the way back I balance the heavy load and pace myself. My muscles tire. After trudging about a third of the way back, I stop and relax. My muscles renew themselves, and in a few moments I am ready to take up my burden again. I do not wait until I get back to the cabin to relax: I relax right then and there.

To adapt an old saying, "An ounce of renewal is worth a pound of effort." And what is true of muscles is, likewise, true of the mind. The strength of the mind can be renewed through relaxation.

RESTING Relaxing is resting. Resting is not the same as renewing. To rest means to turn one's attention to some-thing other than the problem. Resting means distracting, putting one's mind at rest, thinking about a different issue. Although we may not realize it at a given moment, there is more to us than the stress we are experiencing in whatever predicament has been preoccupying us. To rest means to put the mind at rest, if only for a moment; to let it flitter away from the stress of the moment. Learning how to relax often means imagining oneself at a different place, perhaps in a meadow with a flowing brook. To relax means to give the mind a reprieve from its worries in order that the mind may soon return and try again.

RE-CREATING Relaxing means re-creating; finding a new way to solve old problems. Re-creating goes beyond reflecting. Re-creating implies entering again into that unique human capacity, namely, to create novel and unique approaches to the dilemmas of life. Relaxing makes this possible.

Research on experimental neurosis with rats found, in one study, that as the rats became more and more tense due to stronger electric shocks to their feet, their behavior became more and more stereotyped. Their previous learning seemed to disappear, and the ability they had shown to solve new problems faded. Under duress they simply chose one behavior and stuck to it even when there was no reward for doing so; they lost their ability to be creative. When they were given some escape from the stressful situation, their creativity returned. Humans are like that. Relaxation provides the release from stress that people need to be creative again.

REGAINING Relaxing means regaining—regaining the self-esteem often lost in the midst of confrontations, failures, and frustrations. There is always the danger that the stress of life will turn into distress—the feeling that all is lost and that we must fight for our existence. Relaxation provides the space we need to remember that we belong to God and that he loves us. We are, indeed, OK. Once we recall and reexperience this truth, we regain our self-esteem and are able to return to our problems with new vigor and strength. Under stress we tend to forget the foundation on which true self-esteem rests. We become so engrossed in winning the battle or in having others respect our opinion that we inadvertently allow our self-esteem to become intertwined with the predicament we face. Relaxing makes regaining our self-esteem possible.

RESTORING Relaxing means restoring. Restoring is a vibrant term. When things are restored, they look like new.

I have a 1961 Nash Metropolitan automobile and have been restoring it for a decade. It looks good. Often when I am waiting at a stoplight, someone in a neighboring car will call out the window, "What a great car!"

There is a restored look to relaxed persons that cannot be denied. They have learned how, in the very thick of life's battles, to remain relaxed and function as wholesome, holy persons who bring their best selves to the tasks of life. Relaxing restores us, mentally and physically, to our optimal functioning. Even bones are restored. Much of the wear and tear of life is reversed, just as when an old car's paint job is changed to its original luster.

From a Christian point of view, relaxation makes the restoration of the image of God a reality. We become who we were created to be, namely, reflections of God, mirrors of the divine. (And when we sense that happening within us, we won't be too surprised should someone say to us, "You look great.")

REINSTATING Finally, relaxing means reinstating. Reinstating the calm and the courage we lose when stress almost overwhelms us is probably the most important benefit of relaxation. It has been said that abundant life includes three things: someone to love, some job to do, and something to hope for. Reinstating refers to that something to hope for. Relaxing gives us a future. Distress makes us feel there is no way out, no solution, no power, no self-esteem; relaxing reinstates our courage.

For Christians, this is the crux of the matter. Through our relaxing, our identity and status with God are reinstated. We remember what is truly real. We are brought once again into God's love and care. That gives us a future to hope for and the courage to pursue it. This aspect of relaxation should never be discounted or downplayed.

Reflecting, renewing, resting, re-creating, regaining, restoring, reinstating: we can expect all these from learning to relax. But lest you think that relaxation is our complete cure for all ills, let me remind you that we are still fragile human beings. Even at our best, in achievement we only approximate the promise of all that might be ours in relaxation. However, that reality does not in the least detract from the immeasurable fulfillment that will be ours if we put our minds to the task.

There is a delightful little book by Fynn called *Mister God, This Is Anna*. It is replete with the observations of a little London waif who is taken in by a compassionate stranger. Anna says that God's greatest gift is rest. However, she said that God didn't rest because he was tired but because things were "no longer in a muddle." Anna was probably a better theologian than she realized. If relaxation indeed is a gift, as I've claimed, then probably its best result is that things are "no longer in a muddle." A better summation of the "seven Rs" of relaxation would be hard to find.

It should be said, however, that God's rest came after all the work of creation was completed. Our creations fall far short of completion. We need to carry over into our daily lives a relaxed attitude and remember that God knows the limits of our power and strength. He does not expect us to wait to rest until all of our lives are in order and all our work is done. As the Bible states, ''For he knows how we are made; he remembers that we are dust'' (Psalm 103:14). We need frequent periods of relaxation in order to keep the muddle of our lives from becoming overwhelming. Thanks to our allowing relaxation to come into our busy lives, our ''creations'' can be ultimately fulfilled through God's power.

We next consider the viewpoints of the Bible and of science about why it is important for us to relax.

Therefore I tell you,
do not be anxious about your life...
—JESUS (MATTHEW 5:25)

CHAPTER 6

What the Bible Says About Relaxing

The Bible has some definite answers to the question, "Why should we relax?"

Anxiety is the Bible's word for "stress." *Peace* is the Bible's word for "relaxation." Each of these words has an ancient linguistic heritage that makes its meaning very slightly different from today's. However, understanding biblical anxiety and its opposite, peace, is very important to modern-day Christians who want to learn to live calm and confident lives.

The biblical word for anxiety is *merimna*. It is a Greek word that means "drawn in different directions; to be distracted." It is a good translation of the Aramaic word Jesus used in his parable of the farmer who planted grain. Some of the seed the farmer sowed fell on the path, and birds ate it. Some seed fell on rocky ground and died. Some seed fell among thorns and was choked.

ANXIETY: SEEDS THAT FALL AMONG THORNS

Jesus compared the seeds that fell among thorns to anxious people, who, he said, "hear the word, but the cares of the world, and the lure of wealth, and the desire for other things come in and choke the word, and it yields nothing" (Mark 4:19). Note that those seeds amidst the thorns had to fight for their lives. Anxious people act as if they were being attacked by thorns. They, like the seeds of grain, are so preoccupied with the "cares of the world" that they cannot grow. Jesus spoke of their anxiety as "choking the word." By that he meant that their worry so filled their thinking that there was no room left in their minds for the truth of the gospel to enter. And the truth of the gospel is that life can be lived in confidence, security, and, above all, peace.

ANXIETY: BEING DISTRACTED BY
WORLDLY CARE

The same meaning of anxiety can be seen in Jesus' reply to Martha when he was visiting her and her sister Mary. Mary dropped all that she was doing and sat down to talk with Jesus. Martha became troubled and said, "Lord, do you not care that my sister has left me to do all of the work by myself? Tell her then to help me." Jesus answered, "Martha, Martha, you are worried and distracted by many things; there is need of only one thing. Mary has chosen the better part . . ." (Luke 10:40–42).

In effect, Jesus was saying to Martha, "Don't worry about lunch. Don't be concerned about whether the beds are made or the floor is clean. I'm here for a visit. Put those things aside. Come, let's talk with each other." And, literally, "Be relaxed," he said.

The Greek word for relaxation is *amerimnos* and means "freedom from care." That condition is the opposite of stress and worry. Jesus was telling Martha that she was foolishly stressing herself by being so concerned with getting the housework done. She was "choking the word," or strangling the fundamental truth; the truth that she did not need to be anxious about daily matters.

JESUS' TEACHING: BE NOT ANXIOUS

Jesus used the word *amerimnos* in the Sermon on the Mount, saying, "Do not be anxious" (Matthew 6:25). In what Jesus said next he touched on almost everything that we worry or are anxious about; everything we do to attain and defend our self-esteem. Jesus stated that we are not to worry about what we will eat or drink, what clothes we wear, how we appear to others, how long we will live, whether others do us harm or not, whether we are rich or not, whether we get a fair deal from others or not, whether others know we pray or give offerings or go to church at all, whether we are recognized, honored, or rewarded!

Read the entire Sermon on the Mount in Matthew 5, 6, and 7 and see the list of things Jesus included in his do-not-be-anxious catalogue. Little that we value is left out. The list is shocking, even offensive, to our eyes. We have felt that the confidence and calm that Jesus promised came through our own achievements and efforts. But now it seems that we are asked to become defenseless if we are to follow Jesus—to lower our guard; to spend little, if any, time worrying about all those things we thought were absolutely necessary for God's approval and for the safeguarding of our dignity and self-esteem.

The comedian Flip Wilson used to do a routine on his television program as the preacher of "The Church of What's Happening Now." His favorite message was "It don't matter!" Jesus' message in the Sermon on the Mount could be summed up in the same way: "It don't matter!" It's as if Jesus is saying, "All your anxiety is about things that don't matter. More important, all your stress and strain is misplaced. You are trying to live in a briar patch of your own creation where you spend all your energy fighting off thorns instead of putting your roots down into the good earth. Your worries consume your strength. They distract you; they pull your attention away; they cause you to be hypertensive and supervigilant. Your achievements, your reputation, your accomplishments, your possessions, your dignity, your clothes—none of these really matter. So why get so worked up about it all? Why worry about 'laying up for yourselves treasures on earth where moth and rust consume and where thieves break through and steal'? Just relax."

This is radical teaching. However, I do not believe we can reach any other conclusion after reading the Scriptures. I wish I could offer another interpretation, but I don't see how it might be possible to do so. Shortly before he was crucified, Jesus restated his teaching. "Be on guard," Jesus admonished his disciples, "so that your hearts are not weighed down with dissipation and drunkenness and the worries of this life. . . ." (Luke 21:34). Here Jesus made anxiety sound like the confusion and instability that go along with getting drunk and becoming physically ill! What Jesus knew has been confirmed by modern science—stress can make you sick.

JESUS' ANTIDOTE TO ANXIETY AND STRESS

Does Jesus have an antidote to anxiety? To stress? Indeed he does. Instead of distracting ourselves with worry, we are encouraged to "strive first for the Kingdom of God and His righteousness" (Matthew 6:33). Jesus did not equate striving with stress. He simply meant that stress and anxiety arise when we strive for the wrong thing. Striving for the kingdom of God is OK; it results not in stress, but in peace. That's what Jesus meant when he said that becoming anxious with the cares of this world is like trying to grow seeds of grain in a briar patch. People become anxious and stressed because they keep striving over what does not bring peace. Striving for the kingdom of God brings peace. In fact, Jesus boldly added that those who put striving for the kingdom of God first in their lives will have "all those things given to you as well" (Matthew 6:33b).

We have all had the experience of having our anxiety rise as we tried and tried again to solve some problem only to have a flash of insight that we were using the wrong method. It's like trying to get in the front door and suddenly discovering you've been using the back door key; like watching the moments ticking away as you desperately try to solve a math problem on a test and then have a flash of insight as to what you've been doing wrong; like Rue McClanahan in an episode of the TV program "The Golden Girls," in which she belatedly discovered that the man she was dating was interested more in companionship and care in the event that he had a heart attack than he was in sex—which she thought was all he wanted.

Jesus offers us an insight more profound than discovering we've been using the wrong key, been trying the wrong mathematics approach, been misjudging what others wanted in a relationship. He offers a total answer to a universal problem—we all want peace of mind and soul. All of us want to live victorious, secure lives. Jesus' solution: "Strive first for the kingdom of God."

ST. PAUL: THE LAW AND THE SPIRIT

What Jesus spoke of in terms of anxiety and the kingdom of God, St. Paul wrote about in terms of the "law" and the "spirit." Trying to live up to the laws of Moses was the great concern of the scribes and Pharisees. They thought that by stringent obedience to the Old Testament law they could gain the respect of people, and the blessing of God. They tried to fulfill every dietary and worship requirement. Paul declared that this sort of activity is doomed to failure. He called it the "law of sin and death" (Romans 8:2). By this he meant that in trying to gain respect and blessing by frantic efforts to impress others by good behavior, we are on a dead-end street. In the final analysis, it won't work. Paul called this style of living "works righteousness."

Although he used strong words to describe living by "the law," Paul sensitively acknowledged how tempting it is to try to gain security in this way. He wrote about his own struggle in the book of Romans. Once we understand that "living by the law" is as modern as it can be, we realize that Paul was not unlike us though he lived almost two thousand years ago. Our stress-filled attempts to find peace by impressing others and being morally perfect are identical to his. He spoke for us when he wrote:

For we know that the law is spiritual; but I am of the flesh, sold into slavery under sin. I do not understand my own actions. For I do not do what I want, but I do the very thing I hate. Now if I do what I do not want, I agree that the law is good. But in fact it is no longer I that do it, but sin that dwells within me. For I know that nothing good dwells within me, that is, in my flesh. I can will what is right, but I cannot do it. For I do not do the good I want, but the evil I do not want is what I do. Now if I do what I do not want, it is no longer I that do it, but sin that dwells within me.

So I find it to be a law that when I want to do what is good, evil lies close at hand. For I delight in the law of God in my inmost self, but I see in my members another law at war with the law of my mind, making me captive to the law of sin that dwells in my members. Wretched man that I am! Who will rescue me from this body of death? Thanks be to God through Jesus Christ our Lord!

So then, with my mind I am a slave to the law of God, but with my flesh I am a slave to the law of sin.

There is therefore now no condemnation for those who are in Christ Jesus. For the law of the Spirit of life in Christ Jesus has set you free from the law of sin and death (Romans 7:14–8:2).

This is "law-spirit language" at its best! Paul noted how tempting it is to give over our self-esteem to trying to live up to the law—be that law cultural expectation, ethical guidelines, high achievements, or Jewish commandments. He even admitted that he, too, tried hard to win God's and others' favor by desperately attempting to perform well. Finally Paul acknowledged that his efforts failed and that he needed help. He called his stressed, anxious state a "body of death." You can't get much more discouraged than to say "The way I'm living is killing me; I need someone to rescue me."

GOD GIVES US THE VICTORY; LOOK TO JESUS—
HE HAS GRACE

This was the clincher for Paul, and for us, too. In answer to his own plea for help, Paul exclaimed, "Thanks be to God through Jesus Christ our Lord." The Bible's answer to anxiety, worry, and stress can be found in "Jesus Christ our Lord"—his teaching; his life; his death; his resurrection. Paul seemed to be saying, "Listen to Jesus; he knows the way to peace and calm." Paul put it this way: "For the law of the Spirit of life in Christ Jesus has set you free from the law of sin and of death. For God has done what the law, weakened by the flesh, could not do: by sending his own Son in the likeness of sinful flesh . . ." (Romans 8:2–3a). Paul called looking to Jesus "living by the spirit." He contrasted it to "living by the flesh."

Now what does this all mean? When I asked earlier if Jesus had an antidote for our being overconcerned with the cares of the world, I said that Jesus encouraged us to start by seeking the kingdom of God. And what do we find when we seek the kingdom of God? We find "grace." Grace means love. Grace means goodwill. Grace means affirmation. Grace means recognition. Grace means approval. Grace means acceptance. And with grace come calmness and confidence. Our distress lowers; we are at peace. We are a part of the creation that God looked at when Genesis reported, "And God saw everything that he had made and, indeed, it was very good" (1:31).

That is what we find when we strive after or seek the kingdom of God. It is what we see when we look at Jesus. He was the love of God incarnate, in the flesh. As the gospel of John so hauntingly put it: "And the Word became flesh and lived among us, and we have seen his glory, glory as of the father's only son, full of GRACE and truth'' (John 1:14).

I am aware that all this quoting from the Bible and all this talk about the meaning of biblical words are not new to any of you. You might be asking, ''Is there not some simple way to state this truth that will make me really relaxed? What does all this mean to a twentieth century Christian? Tell me how I can apply and use it.''

Theologian and philosopher Paul Tillich places the problem of stress where it really resides, namely, in our desire for love and acceptance. This is what we've been working so hard to achieve. The message of Jesus is that love is ours for the asking. However, one cannot achieve a state of grace by specifically seeking it. Rather, it may come to us precisely at the moment when we have lost faith in ourselves or in others, when we feel abandoned by God, when we have forgotten the meaning of life. Tillich, in his serman ''You Are Accepted,'' asks us to study Paul's Damascus Road experience for an example of how grace was achieved: when Paul was in his darkest moment of despair, feeling distant from God, man, and himself, his own acceptance of the picture of Jesus as the Christ granted him an overwhelming sensation of being reunited with all to which he belonged. Paul did not receive a solution to his problems, but attained a peace of mind and spirit which could lead him out of his troubles. So, says Tillich, we may experience a similar feeling in modern times:

''. . . it is as if a voice were saying: 'You are accepted . . . accepted by that which is greater than you. . . . Do not try to do anything now; perhaps later you will do much. Do not seek for anything; do not perform anything;

do not intend anything. *Simply accept the fact that you are accepted.''*

To experience grace is to know deep down in our hearts that God loves us, cares for us, and accepts us. The childhood song puts it profoundly and simply: ''Jesus loves me, this I know; For the Bible tells me so. Little ones to him belong. They are weak but he is strong.'' And we could add, ''Not only little ones belong to him, but big ones, old ones, fat ones, tall ones, Americans, Russians, Iranians, Jews, Palestinians, Africans, everybody!'' As the best-known Bible verse concludes, ''For God so loved the world that he sent his only son, that whosoever believes in him should not perish but have eternal life'' (John 3:16).

THE ANTIDOTE TO STRESS—EXPERIENCE THE GRACE OF GOD

To experience the ''grace of God'' is to be rescued from perishing; to discover a life that is better than life at its best. To experience grace is to find the antidote to stress. To experience grace is to encounter the love of God that Jesus taught and that he exemplified by his life and death. To experience the grace of God is to live life on a firm foundation that will not move in the midst of the strongest earthquake or the most violent storm, as Jesus noted in his parable of houses built on sand and rock (Matthew 7:24–27).

To experience grace is to see in Jesus the way life is truly to be lived—by confident faith in God. Even during his travail in the Garden of Gethsemane, when he was about to be crucified, Jesus exclaimed, ''Not my will, but thine be done'' (Mark 14:26). Jesus lived what he preached. He trusted God even though it cost him his life. The stress he felt was not so much the ordeal of his trial and crucifixion as it was in the fear that he would not do God's will. As the Scriptures promise,

> Thou will keep him in perfect peace,
> whose mind is stayed on thee,
> because he trusts in thee.
> Trust in the Lord for ever,
> for the Lord God
> is an everlasting rock. (Isaiah 26:3–4)

JESUS IS WHO WE ARE; HE IS OUR EXAMPLE

Yes, listening to, looking at, and copying Jesus are the Bible's answer to the stress of life.

Another great theologian, Karl Barth, said it simply and directly: ''Jesus is who we are.'' We can look around and compare ourselves to other people, but that will make us like seeds that fight against thorns to live. That will distract and stunt us. In fact, comparing ourselves to others is unreal. The meaningful comparison is Jesus Christ. It is to him that we are to look if we would see how life is to be lived. He is our example, and we are to put our faith and truth in him if we would find peace and freedom from anxiety.

The Scriptures imply that living with faith in God is the natural way. That life is the norm, not the exception. It is how we were created to be from the very beginning. We feel stress when we strive so hard to impress others because all that striving is not natural. Jesus lived the natural life, and that is why Barth said that Jesus is who we are. When we put aside our attempts to perform perfectly—when, instead, we put our faith in God, as Jesus did—then peace will come. That is the way God intended things to be; that is the way he created us to be. After all, we were created as mirrors, or images, of him.

This is the meaning of Jesus' invitation to "Come unto me, all you who are weary and carrying heavy burdens, and I will give you rest. Take my yoke upon you, and learn of me; for I am gentle and humble in heart, and you will find rest for your souls. For my yoke is easy, and my burden is light" (Matthew 11:28). Using the example of a master driving oxen, Jesus invites us to become a part of his and God's wagon team. He tells us to quit working for other masters, pulling other loads; with them we have become weary with the heavy burden of anxious living.

He encourages us to put on the harness of faith. He invites us to put his "yoke" around our necks and begin to pull the "good news" wagon. He assures us that when we work for him, we will find the yoke well padded; we will find our pulling eased when we wear that harness of faith around our necks. God made it to fit us perfectly.

By these words of scripture, Jesus tells us that faith in God eases the stress of life. Our lives are intended to be lived in the consciousness of an inner peace that is ours by God's grace. This is the Bible's answer to why we should relax.

Life with God leads to security and peace. It is a quality of life that cannot be bought or earned. It comes as a gift to those who ask for it.

In another chapter we'll look into how this gift works. For now, however, the Bible's basic answer is that anxiety, worry, and strain are shortsighted. They lead to a stress-filled living that does not afflict people who follow Jesus. For as he said, ''I came that they may have life and have it abundantly'' (John 10:10).

And with that assurance uppermost in mind, we turn to the realm of science for some specifics about the dynamics of stress and relaxation.

CHAPTER 7

What Science Says About Relaxing

The Bible's answers to the question "Why should we relax?" are nearly two thousand years old. The answers of science to the same question began to appear only in the early 1940s. Before then, it seems, nobody thought stress was a problem. People may have lived their lives in "quiet desperation" (Thoreau), but no one else knew it.

However, when science sees a problem, it wastes little time in trying to solve it; we should be thankful for that. Since the time of Sir Isaac Newton, scientists have devoted much of their energy to making life better. The Royal Society of Science in England, of which Newton was a founding member, stated as its purpose "the discovery of the laws of God in nature and the alleviation of human suffering." Modern science's efforts to solve the problem of stress are a continuation of that great tradition. The recommendation that people should relax is based on science's discoveries about the dangers that too much stress can bring.

70

Science has concluded that stress can make you sick as well as shorten your life. Thus, preventing illness and death is science's answer to why we should relax. Health and longevity are the goals.

HEART DISEASE

Chief among the problems stress has brought has been the rise in heart diseases. Early in this century heart problems were less common than they are now. Although they are now the leading cause of death, at the turn of the century heart diseases ranked only fourth. Today they kill more people than all other causes of death put together, including cancer.

How is this rise in heart disease related to science's admonition that we should relax? A leading psychologist, whose name happens to be Hart, answers it this way: "The heart is the central target of destruction for much of the harmful stress that we experience."[1] Mainly, stress harms the heart by causing it to overwork. Archibald Hart diagramed the process; see Figure 2.

When you look at Hart's diagram, you might say, "Why the heart? It appears that stress first affects the brain. Doesn't it wear out, too? Why focus on the heart?" The answer is that the brain does not seem to deteriorate with overuse, but the heart does. Often, fortunately, we can repair or even replace the heart when it wears out; but so far, repairing a damaged brain is tricky, next to impossible. A heart that is forced to pump blood too hard and too fast will simply wear out. When that happens, blood is cut off from vital organs, and they, too, fail to function. It is the heart that is damaged by stress—not, initially, the brain, despite the brain's being the part that tells us we are tense, anxious, worried, and

FIGURE 2
The Stress Response

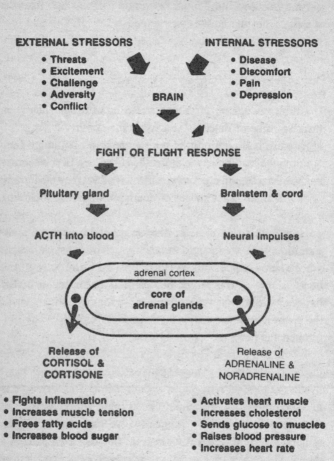

EXTERNAL STRESSORS
- Threats
- Excitement
- Challenge
- Adversity
- Conflict

INTERNAL STRESSORS
- Disease
- Discomfort
- Pain
- Depression

BRAIN

FIGHT OR FLIGHT RESPONSE

Pituitary gland

Brainstem & cord

ACTH into blood

Neural impulses

adrenal cortex

core of
adrenal glands

Release of
CORTISOL &
CORTISONE

Release of
ADRENALINE &
NORADRENALINE

- Fights Inflammation
- Increases muscle tension
- Frees fatty acids
- Increases blood sugar

- Activates heart muscle
- Increases cholesterol
- Sends glucose to muscles
- Raises blood pressure
- Increases heart rate

Reprinted with permission from A. D. Hart, *The Hidden Link Between Adrenaline and Stress*, p. 36.

stressed! The brain sends messages for all parts of the body, and the heart does the work, just as a football coach sends in a play that the quarterback executes.

Just how does the brain respond to stress? The diagram explains the process. The brain perceives that we are being challenged, resisted, harassed, threatened, attacked, or confronted. It automatically reacts defensively to protect us. The brain decides to stay and struggle with the enemy or retreat to a safer place.

This mechanism is called the "fight or flight" response. It's as if we are sitting quietly in our rocking chair when suddenly a robber bursts in the front door. The brain assesses the situation and quickly determines whether we should stand up and fight or get up and run. As far as the heart is concerned, it matters little whether we defend ourselves or surrender; the extra energy that either decision takes means extra work. If the brain did not have the heart to rely on, we would just sit there and do nothing. The heart provides the energy and means by which we act.

WHY THE HEART WORKS SO HARD

Science has discovered how the heart gets the message that it is to move from slow to high gear. The first signal the brain sends is chemical. The pituitary gland secretes a hormone into the blood. This hormone, called ACTH (adrenocorticotropic hormone), in turn stimulates the adrenal glands. The adrenal glands are also prompted into action by a nerve impulse from the spinal cord. Then the adrenal gland sends a message to the heart.

Thus the brain and the heart have an intermediary. The adrenal gland acts somewhat like a translator between two parties speaking different languages. But here the translation is an order: the hormones that the adrenal gland secretes act to raise the blood pressure, activate the heart muscle, send glucose (sugar) to the muscles, and increase the heart rate.

This process is somewhat like my use of an electric weed-eater at my mountain cabin. The weed-eater is connected to a gas generator that idles along in a gentle hum until I press a hand throttle. This signal passes to the generator along a fifty-foot cord. Immediately the motor revs up, and the generator's hum changes to a loud throb. The cord is to the generator what the adrenal gland is to the heart. My decision to use the weed-eater to cut the grass would be futile if I did not have the power of the generator. And the generator would not respond, no matter how loud I shouted at it, unless the cord carried my message to it. Understanding this link of the brain to the heart through the adrenal gland will become important when we consider science's answer to the question "How can we relax?" Some procedures will involve learning not only how to control the brain's reaction to stress but also how to slow down the excretion of adrenaline and noradrenaline, those hormones that suddenly provoke the heart to work harder.

THE GENERAL ADAPTATION SYNDROME

Blood is to the body what gasoline is to an automobile. It energizes the whole body—in both danger and affection. Blood, in danger, provides the energy for the brain to think, the legs to run, the arms to swing, the eyes to squint, the liver to secrete sugar, the senses to become more acute, the fists to hit. The whole body becomes prepared for defensive action because the heart beats harder and faster. Blood pressure increases. The brain requires more blood to plan reactions. The muscles require more blood to help the body stand up and fight or make a quick retreat. The stomach demands extra blood to convert food into energy. The heart pumps faster and stronger. Like an army battalion that is ordered to battle stations, the heart jumps into action when it receives a command from the brain.

So far as I have described them, those reactions of the heart to stress are natural and normal. As Hans Selye pointed out in his book *The Stress of Life*, to live means to do some things, to act in some ways, to achieve some goals, to meet some challenges, to overcome some problems, to win some battles. Whenever we do such things, we are under tension. We have to exert ourselves to some degree to live. No one goes through life without experiencing stress. It "comes with the territory." This process is called the General Adaptation Syndrome, a widely used term that Selye coined.

As a normal, everyday condition of adjustment, the General Adaptation Syndrome is not destructive. This kind of routine stress has been termed eustress, the "eu" standing for the Greek "good." You may recall that I have termed this condition "success tension." The General Adaptation Syndrome becomes harmful, however, when it occurs too often, lasts too long, and is too extreme. When this happens, the heart has to beat too hard, too long, too often. The heart begins to think that stress is its natural state. It stays revved up like a motor that idles too fast because the choke is stuck or the throttle is pulled out too far. These hearts never relax. Eustress becomes distress.

Several things occur. First, the heart, like any muscle, needs rest to recoup its energy. When it doesn't get its needed rest, it becomes fatigued and strained, just as biceps that lift a weight too many consecutive times become weak and limp. Second, when the heart has to work overtime and becomes fatigued, it has to call on a deeper reservoir of energy, which cannot be replaced.

Third, when the hormones of the adrenal gland are secreted, too often they can harm our circulation by causing an overproduction of blood cholesterol. This produces plaque, which narrows the vessels that carry blood to the heart muscle. This cholesterol decreases the ability of the body to remove these harmful blood deposits. Hart concluded: "In short bursts, elevated adrenaline is *not* damaging or dangerous, but when sustained at high levels over a period of time it can be very harmful. Adrenaline arousal can be compared to revving up an engine and then leaving it to idle. Idling an engine on high for a short time clears out gum deposits and dirty carbon. But when the engine is left idling for a long time, carbon deposits collect in the valves. The engine wears out faster."[2]

WEAR AND TEAR DISEASES

These processes result in "wear and tear" disease—premature aging. People who have been under too much strain and stress often have chronological ages that are far younger than their physiological ages. Selye found that this effect was due to too-early draining of limited, irreplaceable bodily reserves:

Apparently, there are two kinds of adaptation energy: the superficial kind, which is ready to use, and the deeper kind, which acts as a sort of frozen reserve. . . . It is the restoration of the superficial adaptation energy from the deep reserves that tricks us into believing that the loss has been made good. . . . Many people believe that, after they have exposed themselves to very stressful activities, a rest can restore them to where they were before. This is false . . . each exposure leaves an indelible scar, in that it uses up reserves of adaptability that cannot be replaced.[3]

These scars mount up. They eventually mean that the heart has no more energy to function and, like a car that is out of gas or an engine that has burned up all its oil, the heart breaks down.

The idea that each of us has only a limited amount of "frozen reserve" adaptation energy that cannot be replaced once it is used up runs counter to what most people—particularly young people—have thought. Youth find it difficult to think they will die. Even aging people who sometimes say they are "worn out" may suppose that all they need is more rest; they have not realized that they are nearing exhaustion of their reserves.

Like many Americans who live in the desert southwest with little concern over the water supply there despite the constant danger of a shortage, many people have ignored voices such as Selye's.

In a sense, adaptation energy is like the world's fossil fuel. Like oil, adaptation energy is each individual's precious commodity. If not conserved, it is always in danger of being exhausted too quickly and too early in life.

This is where learning to relax comes in. Relaxing is a process of pacing oneself so that dipping into one's energy reserves does not occur casually or unnecessarily. Relaxing is also a process of intentionally slowing the body down after it has been under stress. Selye states these steps poignantly with these words: "True age depends largely on the rate of wear and tear, on the speed of self-consumption; for life is essentially a process which gradually spends the given amount of adaptation energy that we inherited from our parents. Vitality is like a special kind of bank account you can use up by withdrawals but cannot increase by deposits. Your only control over this most precious fortune is the rate at which you make your withdrawals."[4]

So the obvious answer of science to the question "Why should we relax?" is "To increase our life span." From one viewpoint, this answer would seem to be entirely quantitative, as if life can be measured entirely in terms of length or number of years. "Life span" surely means more than that; but it is certainly true that one cannot enjoy life if one is not alive!

Selye noted that he had never known anyone to die of old age if by "old age" one meant that all body parts wore out at the same time. What caused death, according to Selye, was the wearing out of one body part, for example the heart, essential to the coordination of all the rest of the body.

Science's goal would probably be that we all die of old age when all parts of the body wear out at the same time. Until that becomes possible, the reason for relaxing is to approximate that goal and maintain as much tenacity and vitality in the organs affected by stress, so that we can live longer and live with as few handicaps as possible. Happiness as well as longevity is the goal. Certainly the incapacity that results from strokes, heart attacks, ulcers, and chronic pain are to be avoided if at all possible. To live with such stress-causing (and, sometimes, stress-caused) diseases can seem as bad as death.

STRESS ADDICTION

Surely, most people would like to get rid of stress if it resulted in illness or death. Yet, strangely enough, some people have become addicted to stress. They encourage it and like it. Stress has become a way of life. Being "stressed out" has become the rule, not the exception. They feel that if they did not maintain a hyperalert, defensive stance, they would not keep up with life, and perhaps other people would take advantage of them.

I know a property owner who visits her rental property at least twice a month and goes through her renters' homes when they are not at home just to be sure her houses are not being destroyed. She stands over all repair people and challenges their every move. One plumber said to her, "I don't think you trust me." He was right. She doesn't trust him or anybody else, for that matter.

She is an immigrant who has worked tirelessly to make it in America and who has had a hard life. That she is overdefensive and confrontational makes some sense in light of her history. However, she represents many people who feel just as she does; they feel that if they let down their guard for a moment, they will lose everything. Yet, if science is correct, her body is taking a beating with constant oversecretion of adrenaline, heightened blood pressure, hyperacidity in her stomach—not to mention her constant worrying and the threats to her welfare that, generally, don't materialize. She may already experience some arthritis, headaches, and high cholesterol; I do not know.

An emotional disturbance called "Post Traumatic Stress Disorder" (PTSD) sometimes affects people who have been through such turmoil as she has in escaping from Russia.

But usually people suffering from PTSD wish to get rid of the past. They do not nurse, harbor, and indulge it, as she seems to do.

Science knows that the results of constant stress are highly predictable. In fact, being overly tense for prolonged periods of time has been called the "silent killer." Many people live stressed lives and think that all their problems are outside them. But their bodies are aging prematurely, and some parts may break down long before they should. Then these overstressed people will be left with broken-down body parts or terminal illnesses. These days, even cancer is being partially attributed to too much stress.

Researchers and doctors have also observed that many people have become addicted to the stimulation and excitement they feel when they are tense. They do not feel alive when they are relaxed. Stress attracts them the way honeysuckle attracts a bee. They are bored when they are not excited. They seem proud to say they never get enough sleep.

Psychologist Hart calls these people "adrenaline addicted." They self-consciously and intentionally seek stress so that they can experience the invigoration that comes when adrenaline is secreted. They enjoy stress. Many people report that they never felt more alive than when they were in a good fight, solving a nearly insurmountable problem, or sailing during a storm at sea. Those reports are examples of the alertness, the excitement, and the stimulation that many people seek today. Thrill-seeking is a byword for much of modern living, and stress is often a non-drug way many persons seek to overcome the boredom and lethargy they feel. Stress, which should be an experience to avoid, has become an experience to seek.

I have a friend who has lived his whole life courting

stress. He has a saying, "Better to burn out than to rust out." He is now in his late fifties. I marvel that his body has held up as well as it has. He constantly gives himself one stressful challenge after another. He is an entrepreneur who sets up educational tours to China, speaks to industrialists in New York, cultivates corn on a farm in the southeast, coordinates the importing of goods from Singapore, fights for causes he believes in, challenges retailers who might cheat him, sets deadlines he can never meet, *and* tries to do all these things at once! He is never where he says he will be. His causes are many; his interests are diverse. He will sit still for a half hour at most. Then he must be going—somewhere, someway, somehow. He lives off an adrenaline high. He never relaxes.

He reminds me of reports about the founder of the Methodist Church, John Wesley. Wesley was up at 4:00 A.M. every day and worked ceaselessly, speaking or writing, until late into the night. He never settled down but traveled from place to place in England until his death. He, too, was addicted to stress.

Although Wesley lived to eighty-eight, science tells us that many stress addicts will pay a toll for their behavior. Their bodies cannot help but wear out prematurely. Alas, a good many stress addicts have not heard the message and will have to get worse before they get better. Alcoholics Anonymous has been familiar for years with that sad dynamic of human behavior.

The message of science is that stress should be experienced in moderation—not in excess. It is abnormal and unhealthy to live in such a way that one is under constant pressure or experiences persistent threat. Science insists that while there is much in modern life to cause us stress, there is also much that we can do about it. We don't need to be as hypertense as we have thought. Relaxation is a possibility; whether it becomes an actuality is up to us. Carl Rogers, the late psychologist, suggested that life should be lived with "just manageable anxiety." Science would probably agree. Life should be lived with "just manageable" stress if one desires health and longevity.

1. Hart, A.D. *The Hidden Link Between Adrenaline and Stress* (Waco, Texas: Word Books, Inc., 1986).
2. *Ibid.*, pp. 38–39.
3. Selye, H. *The Stress of Life* (New York: McGraw Hill, 1956, 1976), p. 429.
4. *Ibid.*, p. 428.

He who has a how to live,
can live through any why.
—FRITZ PERLS

CHAPTER 8

How We Should Relax:
First Steps

Having a *why*, or purpose, for living makes our acting to survive bad situations, the *how* of life, bearable. Viktor Frankl proved that in *From Death Camp to Existentialism*, his story of how he survived imprisonment in a Nazi concentration camp. Yet, having a *how*, or method, for handling stressful situations is just as important as always knowing *why* one is under pressure, what stress does to the body, or whether Christians should relax.

Take the case of a man who was attacked with a baseball bat and a hammer over a traffic confrontation. In the summer of 1990, the news reported the story of that man. He got out of his car and began to yell at another driver, who had cut him off in a turn. When the offending car began to pull away, the antihero of our story shouted, "Come back, you SOB!" And return the "SOB" did—with a vengeance. Two of the car's occupants got out and added injury to insult, beating their victim so badly with a baseball bat that he had to go to the hospital. In addition the assailants broke out the headlights and taillights of his car before they left! This man had needed a method for handling his stress; that is, he'd needed a *how*. His reason for yelling at the other car—his *why*—got him into more trouble than he bargained for. He had a good *why*, but a poor *how*!

This chapter presents a *how*, a basic method for reducing stress. I call this method "First Steps in Relaxation." There are four steps: Pull Back, Simmer Down, Loosen Up, and Focus In. If the battered man whose car was cut off had possessed such a method, he might have avoided the hospital and have still-intact headlights and taillights to boot!

PULL BACK

When we are feeling stressed, pulling back from the situation a bit is a crucial first step to take. There is no substitute for pulling back. Pulling back means what it says; taking hold and dragging yourself away from the predicament.

Much of the pressure we feel stems from our imagining that we are glued to whatever situation we are experiencing. We do not feel we can get unstuck, so we just continue to worry about our problem. We bang on a door that does not open and think we have no alternative but to continue banging until our knuckles are bruised and bleeding. Only rarely does it occur to us to simply step back from the door for a moment, to pause for thought. Imagine a runner meeting up with a brick wall. Instead of continuing to run head-on into the wall again and again, or giving up and returning home, the runner steps off to the side of the path and puzzles over the situation.

Stepping back is distinctly different from the tendency

we feel toward "fight or flight" when we feel stressed. We find a good example is the problem many people have in going to sleep at night. Dr. Arthur Spielman, director of the Sleep Disorders Center at the City College of New York, reports that people commonly try too hard to sleep or give up too easily. Thus, they spend endless hours trying to get to sleep or they refuse to get into bed because they think they cannot sleep. He recommends neither alternative. Better that people step back from the problem, not try so hard, get their minds on other tasks. Dr. Spielman concludes that regardless of what they say, most people get enough sleep if they have enough energy to do their daily tasks.

Pulling back is a skill. It is not an instinct. Pulling back does not happen automatically. It will not occur without self-conscious intention. It involves, first, a clear-cut realization that one is tensed up and under pressure. This realization is followed by an awareness that the tension will only increase with the passage of time—in other words, things will get worse rather than better. Then, a further discovery occurs: one is able to consciously back away from the situation; one is not inexorably stuck in the tension. Finally, this realization leads to a determination to actually *get* some breathing space. Then, and only then, can one truly pull back.

An example from my teaching experience illustrates how pulling back results from a determined decision.

I teach in a graduate school. At the conclusion of every course I teach, students fill out an evaluation form. I try to do my best, and I hope they will like the course. About four weeks into the next term, I receive a summary of these student evaluations. When I take the envelope marked "course evaluations" out of the mailbox, I begin to feel tense. I am aware that, try though I may, I have not always pleased students in the past. I open the evaluations with some trepidation. I can feel my heart beat faster, my throat catch a bit, and my palms begin to sweat. I remember one course I taught on adult counseling after which a student wrote on his evaluation, "This professor needs counseling." I always worry about what I will find written in these evaluations. In the past I have managed to please the majority of students, but the criticisms of some students have left me sensitive and wary.

I should have gotten accustomed to various reactions to how I teach by now. After all, I have been a college professor for over twenty-five years. I am surprised that I still tense up when I look at these student evaluations each term. The last time I picked up the envelope I decided to try a different tack, however. I realized my stomach was tightening, and I was becoming anxious. However, I determined to pull back from the situation. I took a deep breath and said to myself, "This is not the end of the world; you will make it through this." It worked. My determination did not change the ratings. As a matter of fact, the criticisms were some of the worst I've ever gotten. But I got some breathing space just by making a conscious decision to pull back.

Pulling back is tantamount to stepping aside for a brief time and catching one's breath. It recalls to us an admonition of generations of parents to their children: "Count to ten before you speak." In pulling back we are distracting ourselves a bit. Pulling back provides the time to put the other three steps into action. Without that time and mental freedom, the other three steps—simmering down, loosening up, and focusing in—will never occur. That is what makes pulling back such a crucial and important step.

Before we go further, we should remind ourselves again that pulling back is a skill, not a talent one is born with.

But we should not forget that all skills are based on abilities. We *can* step back; we have that ability. It is a dormant ability that must be honed into a skill. Nevertheless, pulling back is a possibility that, with practice, can become a probability.

I recommend that at first you practice pulling back in situations that involve your being under only a little stress. Think about the situation and consciously pull back from it. For a brief moment reflect on your involvement; then pull away from the pressure for an instant. Do that often enough, and you will have acquired the skill that will be the foundation for the other steps to follow. Relaxation becomes a possibility now that you have provided yourself the mental space to make it happen.

SIMMER DOWN

The second step in relaxing is to "simmer down." Simmering down follows "pulling back" and is dependent on it. We can simmer down only *after* we have pulled back. It may seem to you that my approach is too elementary; that I do not need to reemphasize this point about the sequence of these steps. But my experience tells me that far too many people try to talk themselves out of stress before they have pulled back from the situation. That doesn't work. To say to yourself, "Calm down now; take it easy; don't get upset; just relax," while you remain firmly attached to the situation is to doom yourself to failure. Unless you have first gone through the process of realizing you can get some mental distance from the event and have taken the pull-back step to achieve some breathing room, you will not relax.

I once counseled a couple who were having marital difficulties. As we started to talk, they began to berate and accuse each other. Their voices rose, and their eyes flashed. They were both becoming extremely stressed as they defended themselves from each other's accusations. I made the mistake of intervening with these words: "Now, will both of you just calm down?" The husband answered me with words that were entirely correct and put me in my place. He said, "How can I calm down when she is saying those things about me?"

He was right. I was wrong. He couldn't calm down just because I ordered him to do so. Although neither of us knew it at the time, he could calm down only after he had pulled back. Only after he had realized that he was not entirely a victim of the situation and had mentally caught his breath for a moment would it be possible for him to calm down to any degree. And what was true for him was also true for his wife.

Having remade this point about simmering down following pulling back, let's answer the question "What does it mean to simmer down?" To simmer down means to turn the heat down. It does not mean to turn the heat off. When Flip Wilson did his routine in which he preached "It don't matter!" he meant "cool off"—but don't *turn* off completely. Things *do* matter. When we are experiencing stress, it is unrealistic to think we can get rid of all the anxiety we are feeling just by saying "It don't matter." Saying that things don't matter (like saying we can turn the heat all the way off) would mean denial. Denial of reality is neither possible nor healthy.

But it is possible, realistic, and healthy to think that we can lower our feelings to a *degree*. If by "heat" we mean the tension and strain we feel when we are under pressure, to simmer down implies that we lower the hot stress we are experiencing; that we turn it down, not off. My experience with student evaluations is but one example.

Simmering down needs to be distinguished from the next step, loosening up. Simmering down is something one does with one's mind. Loosening up is something one does with one's body. Both are important, but simmering down must go before loosening up. From my explanation of how the brain sends messages to the heart, it should be clear that the body responds to the mind, not vice versa. (That is true far more often than not; sometimes it can be made to apply even when we are experiencing bodily pain.)

To simmer down the mind means to decatastrophize the experience. When we are under stress, we have probably given the situation too much power and assumed that we were in a life-and-death crisis. Thus, our minds have sent messages to our body to get ready to fight for life! Were that true it would, indeed, be a catastrophe. But that is usually not the case.

I do not mean to imply that there are no situations in which our very existence is threatened. There are. James Loder recounts one such event in his book *The Transforming Moment*. He and his family were in a terrible automobile accident. He found that his wife was pinned under the car. With unexplainable and inordinate strength, he lifted the car off her body. Later it became apparent that his achievement had, seemingly, surpassed human possibility. He did not know how he had done it. The only explanation was that he experienced the moment as life-and-death stress, and his body revved up to the demands it required.

Most of the stresses we experience are not life-and-death. Our tension is often more than is needed to face the crisis. Simmering down is, in part, this realization that "the tension does not fit the crime"; we are more upset than we need to be. Again, this is not to say, along with Flip Wilson, that "it don't matter." It is to say, "I am not in as much danger as I thought; I will survive; I don't need to be as upset as I am; I can come off the stress a bit." The phrase "a bit" in this last sentence is the key. We can simmer *down* but not turn the heat *off*.

All of us have had people break in line at the bank or push ahead of us as we waited for our bags to come down the chute at the airport. We feel like demanding our rights and telling those people to wait their turn. Just a little simmering down will convince us, however, that "the punishment may not fit the crime." We usually get up to the bank teller only a few minutes later than we would have, and getting our bags in timely fashion doesn't seem to depend on where we are standing. My father-in-law once reminded me that the difference between traveling at seventy-five miles per hour and staying within the speed limit of fifty-five miles per hour was getting to my destination ten minutes earlier. That kind of advantage is not worth the extra pressure (and risk) it takes to drive the car at a high speed!

Flip Wilson may have been wrong to proclaim, "It don't matter," but he would have been right had he said, "It don't matter as much as you thought it did." We do tend to exaggerate; the threat to our existence is less than at first we thought. As the popular song puts it, "A country boy can survive." So can city folk! Simmering down assures us that's true.

Some time ago I had the experience of simmering down. I was riding the bus from Seattle, Washington, to Portland, Oregon. My trip took place during a bus strike. That was my first frustration. Strikers walking a picket line blocked our path and caused us to leave an hour late. The driver was a substitute who didn't know the route. We arrived in Portland two hours behind schedule. I was anxious because

I could not forewarn my son, who had come out of a sickbed to meet me. My greatest frustration came, however, from the young woman sitting behind me. She was playing on her portable stereo some of the most bouncy music I had ever heard. Although she was using earphones, she had the volume turned up so high that rows of travelers all about her were exposed to the heavy beat of the drums and snatches of the melody; there was not one letup during the trip. My tension mounted. I suddenly became aware that I was sitting rigidly in my chair. My jaws and my fists were clenched.

I could have moved away from her—except that there was no place to move to. The bus was full. Or I could simply have asked her to turn the music down. But she seemed to be enjoying it so much that I decided against it. Instead, I decided to simmer down. I pulled back from the predicament and talked to myself. I asked myself, "What is happening to you? Are you being physically harmed? Are you being emotionally abused irreparably? Are you going to be crazy after you get off this bus?" My answer to each of these questions was "No." "Then what is going to happen?" I asked myself. "You are going to be inconvenienced, disturbed, hemmed in for four hours. That's bad, but it is not catastrophic. It will end. You can stand it," came the answer. I sat back and relaxed. I turned my mind to other things. No, the irritating music did not go away, but I defused the situation to the degree that I was no longer as upset and stressed about it as I had been.

The difference between the degree of pressure we are experiencing when we step back and the lower tension we experience when we simmer down is the key to relaxing. Often this difference is just enough to give us the space we need to go on to the next step and calm down our bodies.

LOOSEN UP

When I bought a diesel-powered car, I was told that sometimes they continued to run even when you took your foot off the accelerator. That can be dangerous, to put it mildly. Our bodies are like those out-of-control diesel cars. In fact, tension-filled bodies *will* remain tense even after we simmer down. To think that simmering down will automatically make our bodies relax is a gross error. It will not work that way. We have to intentionally loosen up our bodies or they will take on a life of their own. Many people who never knew they had high blood pressure or muscle tension have discovered that truth when they went to the doctor for a sore throat or some other unrelated infection.

One of the most revolutionary discoveries that science has made in the last quarter century is that we *can* loosen up our tense bodies! We can master the technique of deep muscle relaxation. We can learn biofeedback procedures designed to reverse the ill effects of the adrenal glands on our heart and muscles. Once it was thought that the reaction of the adrenal and pituitary glands to threat was automatic and out of conscious control, but we now know that is not true. The alarm reactions of the sympathetic and parasympathetic nervous systems can be reversed. We can intentionally change our tense bodies back to a state of calm. Just as surely as we can pull back from pressure and simmer down by rethinking the predicament we are in, so we can loosen up our bodies by using well-known techniques. Let me describe some of them. They will work! All it takes is practice.

First of all, tense up all the muscles of your body by scrunching your toes, bending your legs, tightening your stomach, clenching your fists, flexing your biceps, gritting your teeth, arching your neck, clamping shut your eyes, and holding your breath. This may sound crazy. How can you loosen up your body by making it more tense? The answer is that you must force yourself to become aware of the tension in order to gain a reasonably accurate sensation of what it might mean to relax. By tensing your whole body you accentuate the tension and make it worse than it actually is.

After you hold your body as tense as you can for as long as you can, let go. Release all your muscles. Let your arms and legs and neck hang down limp. Breathe deeply. Open your eyes wide. Let your jaw drop. You will feel your body relax and the muscles smooth out. Often you will experience a tingling at the ends of your fingers and near the tips of your toes. That is the tension flowing out of your body. Continue to breathe deeply, and slowly the loosening up of the tension will unfold more deeply.

Repeat this process several times. By matching exaggerated tension with complete letting go, you will bring the tension of your body under your control. You will feel it happen. Loosening up becomes a reality. Finally, close your eyes gently and enjoy a feeling of calm euphoria. You will become convinced that your body has responded to your control. In fact, you have done something that in the non-distant past most people in the Western world thought impossible: you have intentionally exercised direction over the parasympathetic nervous system. The blood pressure, the muscle tension, and the hyperalertness that were preparing you to fight have now been restrained and reversed.

Put down the book and practice this procedure several times. When you stop and think about loosening up, I can just hear you saying, ''Hey, wait a minute. This will only work if you have time. And time I don't have. Stress slips up on me. I suddenly discover I'm tense when the battle is raging around me. I can't just stop everything and say, 'Please excuse me while I pull back, simmer down, and loosen up.' Your plan seems idealistic and unrealistic.''

If you say that to me, I reply: "Who's kidding whom? I never said it would be easy. Everybody thinks that they are overwhelmed. Welcome to the crowd. And you're right; relaxing does take time and effort. There is no detour you can take. Remember, your instinct is to fight for your life, to get more and more tense. Relaxation is not the natural reaction to stress. It will not be easy.''

I will admit, however, that the more time you have, the more you can relax. Further, I do acknowledge that the ideal would be to actually retreat to another place off the battlefield. Pulling back, simmering down, and loosening up works best when you can shut your eyes and block out the stressful circumstances and work the plan.

Getting some space away from the situation may be easier than you thought, however. In most predicaments it is possible to take a "potty break." You can get away with asking "Where is your restroom? I need to be excused." Rare is the antagonist who would reply, "I'm not going to let you go or tell you where the bathroom is. Stay put. You can't leave!" Most times you can take a potty break. And there is probably no more private, inviolate place in the world than the stall in a public bathroom. It is the pull-back place par excellence! You will not be disturbed. Once the door is closed and the latch secure, you will have the privacy to simmer down and loosen up.

I have a friend who presents workshops to large audiences. He once conducted a training session at a large hotel in Palm Springs, California. During a break he retreated to the bathroom to calm himself down. His tension was so great that he failed to realize he had entered the women's restroom. He secured himself in a stall and set about gaining some control over his stress, completely unaware that women were going and coming in other parts of the restroom. Although he heard women's voices, he was so deep in concentration that they did not register in his mind. One woman noticed his shoes and pants beneath the walls of the stall and told the hotel security guards. After they had emptied the restroom, they went in. Even then they did not forcefully intrude upon him. "Are you about through?" they asked. "In a minute," my friend replied, still unaware that he was in the women's restroom. "Do you know this is the women's restroom?" they queried. "Really! Oh, my goodness. I am embarrassed. I didn't know. I'll be out immediately," my friend exclaimed.

Now the moral of this humorous story is that even under such outlandish conditions as a man in a stall in the women's restroom, there was no intrusion. Bathrooms offer a kind of retreat. We will have privacy there even under extreme conditions.

Nevertheless, even when we take potty breaks, time may be of the essence. Undoubtedly, many times we will feel rushed. Therefore, I want to share a "quickie" method for loosening up that will work moderately well. It is a variation on the method of tightening up and letting go that I described earlier. It goes like this. Take a deep breath and breathe deeply ten times. As you do so, repeat these words to yourself over and over: "calm body, sound mind." Although you may not feel as relaxed as you would if you had the time to spend tensing up and then letting go, you will still feel a sense of euphoria and calm. The deep breathing will slow the body down, and the muscles will automatically dislodge their tightness. Put the book down and practice this procedure a time or two.

FOCUS IN

The fourth part of this "first steps in relaxation" model is to focus in. To focus in means to turn one's attention to an inner reality. This inner reality transcends the stressful situation. It provides a way to look at the situation from a radically different point of view. This part of the model is where the Christian faith comes in. It is so important that I will devote the whole next chapter to it. Before turning to it, review the model up to this point. Practice pulling back, simmering down, and loosening up. See if you can make it work for you.

> Come to me, all of you who are tired and
> carrying heavy loads, and I will give you rest.
> —MATTHEW 11:28

> "Do not be worried and upset," Jesus told them.
> "Believe in God, and believe also in me."
> —JOHN 14:1

> Throw all your worries on him,
> because he cares for you.
> I PETER 5:7

CHAPTER 9

How to Relax: the Faith Formula

A "faith formula" for relaxation is implicit in the three biblical verses quoted above. It is this: come, believe, throw. Come to Jesus; believe in Jesus; throw your worries on Jesus. The result of coming, believing, and throwing is "peace"—the Bible's word for what it means to live the relaxed life. As Jesus stated, "Peace I leave with you: my own peace I give you. I do not give it to you as the world does. Do not be worried and upset; do not be afraid" (John 14:27).

The key words of our formula (come, believe, throw, peace) are not new to those of us who are already Christian; we have heard many sermons using them. However, our familiarity may cause us to think "Ho hum, I've heard all that before." We may need to be reminded of the richness of meaning those words signify. And even when we feel confident that we know their meaning well, we may need to be sure we know how to make the formula work for us.

After all, this is a chapter on *how* to relax from our Christian point of view. A method lies beneath the formula. And that method is what Christians can master. Faith works—it is practical. Relaxed living is possible. Where there is a will, there is indeed a way.

To begin, let's consider the meaning of these words of the faith formula for relaxation. They are important biblical terms that have specific meaning.

COME—THE FIRST WORD IN THE FAITH FORMULA FOR RELAXATION

Take the word "come." The complete statement Jesus made was: "Come to me, all you who are tired from carrying your heavy loads, and I will give you rest. Take my yoke and put it on you, and learn of me, because I am gentle and humble in spirit; and you will find rest. The yoke I will give you is easy, and the load I will put on you is light" (Matthew 11:28–30).

Though we may not find the possibility flattering, in issuing his invitation Jesus may have been thinking of a cattle yard in which oxen are being put together to pull wagons. Imagine the setting. We see several wagons heaped with goods or other material . . . drivers trying to assemble teams of oxen to pull their wagons . . . oxen standing around regarding the loaded wagons and the drivers with no discernible enthusiasm.

At this point in the story, Jesus pulls a switch. Instead of drivers choosing oxen, Jesus has the oxen choosing the wagons they will pull *and* the drivers for whom they will work. Now, anyone who has dealt with oxen knows that at times they have minds of their own. They balk. They will not move. They refuse to pull. They will not turn to the right or to the left. They continue to eat and drink when it is time to get going. But we never assume those beasts have highly developed brains; they are simply stubborn. They are not self-conscious. They do not think like human beings. And never do we conceive that they might choose what wagon they would pull or what driver they might work for. We may not think in such terms, but Jesus did.

And yet, we realize, Jesus places us above oxen; he reminds us that we are intelligent creatures who can choose. He knows that we have memory; that we remember we've pulled heavy loads; that we know which drivers have mistreated us. Jesus sees us as aware that we do not have to pull any more heavy loads or work for cruel drivers anymore.

This is a different sort of cattle yard. In this one, the oxen make the choice—not the drivers. It is as if Jesus were standing by his wagon holding up a sign that reads, "Hear ye! Hear ye! Listen to me, you oxen. Come over here, all you who are tired from carrying heavy loads, and I will give you rest. Try me out. Put on the harness I offer you. See if it doesn't feel comfortable and pull easily. My wagon has a light load. I am a gentle and humble driver. Come and see if what I promise is not true."

We choose. We accept Jesus' invitation or turn it down. The option is ours. We can choose to stay with the heavy loads, the cruel drivers—in other words, the stress we are feeling. We can even try other drivers or different loads, who may turn out to be just as mean or just as heavy as those we're unhappily accustomed to. Or we can choose to come to where Jesus stands.

This involves choice. It involves action. We cannot just look around, think about it, talk about it, plan to do it. We have to do it. We have to *come* to Jesus. We have to walk over to him and take the risk that his promise is true. We have to say, "I'm here. I accept your offer."

There are two critical points to that first word of the faith formula for relaxation. The first is that Jesus will not force himself on us. The second point is that we not only *have* to choose, we *can* choose to come to Jesus. We have that power and that privilege. The first step is ours, not his.

This first step of coming to Jesus is illustrated in the very first chapter of the gospel of John where Philip finds his brother Nathanael and says, "We have found the one of whom Moses wrote in the book of the Law, and of whom the prophets also wrote. He is Jesus, the son of Joseph, from Nazareth." Nathanael answers Philip skeptically: "Can anything good come from Nazareth?" Philip answers, "Come and see." Nathanael comes, as bidden, to see Jesus—and exclaims, "Teacher, you are the Son of God! You are the King of Israel!" (see John 1:43–50). Nathanael is but one of many people throughout the centuries, countless to us but not to Jesus, who have come to him and discovered their coming was not in vain. For stress-filled people of today, the possibility is excellent that they, too, can find rest in Jesus. But they, like Nathanael, must first "come and see."

Building on the model of chapter 8, when people "center in," they have the chance to come to Jesus or simply to focus on their own inner strength. Often, focusing on one's own inner ability to weather the stress is helpful; we are usually more able to handle stress than we think. But although reminding ourselves of our inner strength is good, coming to Jesus is better. Turning from our own strength to a remembrance of Jesus and his love for us is very helpful. It is shelter amid the storm. Often the very core of the stress we are feeling is helplessness and fear of rejection. In Jesus we find acceptance and reassurance above and beyond our own strength. As the Scriptures state, "The eternal God is your dwelling place and underneath are the everlasting arms" (Deuteronomy 33:27). If people come to Jesus, they intentionally and self-consciously think of him, remember his promises, speak his name, offer a prayer for guidance, and center their thinking on God.

BELIEVE—THE SECOND WORD IN THE FAITH FORMULA FOR RELAXATION

The second word in our faith formula is "believe." It, like the first word, "come," is an admonition Jesus made to his followers. The scene is the Last Supper; Jesus is eating with his disciples. Judas has just left to go out and betray his Lord. The rest of the disciples are worried that Jesus may soon leave them. Jesus calms their anxiety with these words: "Do not be worried or upset. . . . Believe in God, and believe also in me. There are many rooms in my Father's house, and I am going to prepare a place for you. I would not tell you this if it were not so. And after I go and prepare a place for you. I will come back and take you to myself, so that you will be where I am" (John 14:1–4).

The disciples have already taken the first step of "coming" to Jesus. They have been with him for the three years of his earthly ministry. Yet Jesus realizes they are greatly worried and upset. He attributes their stress to lack of belief. They have not taken the second step in the faith formula for relaxation. They do not truly believe.

Believe what? It seems preposterous that Jesus would imply that those who had been closest to him did not believe that he was God and that his leaving them was part of God's plan.

Yet that is exactly what becomes apparent a few minutes later, at the Last Supper, when Philip naively requests, "Lord, show us the Father, that is all we need." In other words, Philip was saying, "Our stress, our worries, our anxiety will subside if you will just cut out all this talk, snap your fingers, and make God appear here and now."

Philip was visually oriented. If Jesus disappeared, he would have nothing left. His faith was quite literal and depended on the evidence of his physical senses. He wanted Jesus to produce a flesh-and-blood God to prove his faith was not in vain. Philip was very modern in some important ways. I suppose that many people would take the first step of reducing stress by coming to Jesus but then balk at really believing in him—particularly if Jesus implied he was about to exit the scene.

Jesus answered Philip, and all other anxious doubters from that day to this, by exclaiming, "Whoever has seen me has seen the Father. Why, then, do you say, 'Show us the Father'? Do you not believe, Philip, that I am in the Father and the Father is in me? The words that I have spoken to you . . . do not come from me. The Father, who remains in me, does his own works. Believe me that I am in the Father and the Father is in me" (John 14:9b–11a).

So, believe what? First of all, believe that Jesus speaks for God. Then, believe that God will take care of you. Jesus said, "There are many rooms in my Father's house, and I am going to prepare a place for you. I would not tell you this if it were not so." This is tantamount to promising that when we trust ourselves to God's care, we will not be disappointed. He has a place for us. The result of being a part of God's wagon team will not only be a light load and an easy yoke but a whole new place for restful living.

Yes, the second step in the faith formula for relaxation

is belief; belief that our commitment of ourselves to Jesus will not be in vain. Jesus shows us by his example what it means to truly believe—and how easy it is to doubt. During the last days of his life on earth he went through the same agony that Philip did in wondering whether God could be trusted. In the Garden of Gethsemane, Jesus was in such stress that he sweat drops of blood. He asked God to find another way to demonstrate his love for the world than by having him go to the cross. Yet he came to the point of saying that he would trust God by saying, "Not my will, however, but your will be done" (Luke 22:42b). When he was on the cross, he went anew through that struggle of not knowing whether to believe. He cried out, "My God, My God, why have you forsaken me?" But just at the moment of his death, Jesus renewed his trust and exclaimed to God, "Into your hands I place my spirit" (Luke 23:46).

By his example, Jesus showed us the importance of believing and the dangers of doubting. He was human, just as we are. Yet he showed us how we can triumph by believing in God. As Karl Barth concluded, "Jesus is who we are." Jesus showed us the grandeur and greatness for which we were created. In the final analysis, we were created to believe. And we were created to relax, through believing; to put our trust in God. Jesus showed us who we are and how we are to live.

This is simply another way of saying what I noted in the chapter on the Bible's answer to our question Why should we relax? To say that we can trust God is the same as saying we are accepted by God and precious in his sight. We have status in God's eyes; he thinks highly of us. We have a place in his scheme of things; he even has a room reserved for us. We are accepted by and acceptable to God.

Belief in the trustworthiness of God is like finding a firm

floor on which to stand when a throw rug begins to slip under one's feet. Belief in God's care is like finding a strong door frame that will not crash in the midst of an earthquake. Those who take this second step in the relaxation formula do find the words of the hymn to be true:

> How firm a foundation, ye saints of the Lord,
> Is laid for your faith in his excellent word . . .
> Fear not, I am with thee: O be not dismayed,
> For I am thy God, and will still give thee aid;
> I'll strengthen thee, help thee, and cause thee to stand,
> Upheld by my righteous, omnipotent hand.
> When thro' the deep waters I call thee to go,
> The rivers of woe shall not thee overflow;
> For I will be with thee thy troubles to bless,
> And sanctify to thee thy deepest distress.[1]

In practical terms, when we center in and come to Jesus, the next step is to reaffirm our faith in him. We do that by offering up the humble prayer of St. Thomas: "Lord, I believe, help thou my unbelief" (Mark 9:24). And we make our faith firm by repeating that prayer, as we feel the need of it and until we reconvince ourselves that God is, indeed, worthy of our trust.

THROW—THE THIRD STEP IN THE FAITH FORMULA FOR RELAXATION

The third word in our faith formula is shorthand for First Peter's admonition to us: "Throw all your worries on him, because he cares for you" (5:7). If we believe that God cares for us, then we can take the next step of "throwing" our worries on him. If we use mailing a letter as an illustration, this third step is akin to putting the letter into the mail slot after one has traveled to the post office (the first step, Come) and made the assumption that the U.S. mails can be trusted (the second step, Believe).

However, putting a letter in the mail slot hardly captures the power of the admonition that we "throw" our worries onto God. Throwing implies pulling back and heaving away whatever one has in one's hand with vigor and force. I recently joined some friends in skipping rocks across the Wenatchee River in western Washington. For nearly an hour we picked up one flat rock after another and challenged each other: Who could get the most skips out of a throw across the river? For quite a time after we quit, I could feel the shoulder tension that came from the exertion of throwing so many rocks into the river. That's what it means to throw. It is not by any means so gentle as letting a letter fall into a mailbox. Throwing requires energy, intention, and power. You know when you have thrown something away with all your might; your arm hurts. You can't throw something away and still hold on to it. When it leaves your hand, it's gone. Someone joked when we were at the river that we had thrown so many rocks from the bank into the water that surely the channel of the river would be changed!

To throw our worries on God implies active intention, forceful direction, and explicit action. Like flat rocks on riverbanks, our stress must be named, identified, explained, and released unto God. Fuzzy, overgeneral, casual, too-quick, or flippant letting go of our worries will not suffice. We must "throw" our stress onto God.

Being that emphatic and direct in our relationship with God is not as easy as it may sound. Some Christians feel that telling God in specific terms where one feels stressed is being too concrete. They think being specific reflects an overpragmatic use of faith. Although there may be some warrant for being cautious about asking God to solve our problems in definite ways, there should be no objection to our expressing to God our unique, personal experiences and asking him to bring rest to our souls. Jesus was specific about which threat caused him such travail. He asked God to let the cup of his death, which he was about to have to drink, to pass from him. Yet he found peace and relaxation by adding, "Nevertheless, not my will but yours be done." We can be explicit about our stresses, yet entrust ourselves to God's will by "throwing" our worries on him. That is what it means to take the third step in the faith formula for relaxation.

Several years ago my oldest son's wife left him. At that time they had been living in a part of the country distant from my home. He was working hard there to get a business started. They were heavily in debt for a house they had been trying to renovate. Things did not go well for my son after his wife left. He tried renting their house but was unsuccessful. His business did not grow. He had to go to the hospital to rid himself of lice he had caught in the cheap hotel to which he had moved. I worried greatly for him. One night I got explicit with God. I said, "God, I believe you have a plan for my son's life. I am deeply worried about his situation. I feel very helpless. I turn it over to you. Give me some peace from my stress." I became calm and trustful. Although I would have preferred that the business succeed and that he be able to sell his house for a profit, the opposite happened. His business failed, and he lost money on the house. But he survived and I relaxed. I no longer felt stressed. This is a good example of "throwing" my worry onto God and knowing that God cared for me and for my son.

So the faith formula for relaxation is the three-step process of coming, believing, and throwing. When we are stressed by the problems of living, we can (1) come to Jesus, who has promised us that his way of life will not overwhelm us; (2) believe that God is worthy of our trust and will accept us just as we are; and, (3) throw our worries on him and entrust our lives into his plan for us. When we do this, we will experience peace.

PEACE—THE END RESULT OF THE FAITH FORMULA FOR RELAXATION

Peace is one of the chief concerns of the Bible. Peace is referred to over two hundred times in the Old and New testaments. The Bible sometimes speaks of peace as if it is a condition between people, as in the announcement of Jesus' birth ("on earth peace, good will to men," Luke 2:14) or in Jesus' Beatitudes ("blessed are the peacemakers, for they shall be called the children of God," Matthew 5:9). But more often, peace is spoken of as something God gives, not something human beings achieve. For example, Paul states, "And God's peace, which is far beyond human understanding, will keep your hearts and minds safe, in union with Christ Jesus" (Philippians 4:7). One of the last things Jesus said to his disciples before his crucifixion was, "Peace I leave with you; my own peace I give you. I do not give it to you as the world does. Do not be worried and upset; do not be afraid" (John 14:27). This understanding of peace as something God gives is the peace that comes after we follow the steps in the faith formula for relaxation. We can relax because we have peace. We have peace because we are relaxed.

What does peace feel like? It feels like calmness; it feels

like confidence; it feels like security; it feels like serenity; it feels like tranquility; it feels like restfulness. The scripture says that the peace that God gives is not the same kind of peace that the world gives. God's peace surpasses human understanding. I suppose we could say that God's peace makes no sense, in that it is not logical that we could find a calm place in the midst of our stress when that calm, that place, didn't necessarily solve our problems or make things different. But calmness is exactly what God's peace gives to us. The reason God's peace works that way is that it redirects our thinking from the problems that are causing our stress and focuses it on a reality that transcends what can be seen and touched.

This leads me to remind myself and you of the very practical lockstep procedure that ties together this faith formula and the previous chapter. You remember that the first steps in relaxing went as follows:

> Pull Back
> Simmer Down
> Loosen Up
> Focus In

The first three of these phrases refer to logical steps based on a scientific, pragmatic way to relax. The last phrase, Focus In, is where the faith formula works best. After we learn how, intentionally, to "pull back" from the stress of the moment, "simmer down" our minds, adrenal glands, and heart, "loosen up" our muscles from tension and strain—then we can attend to what is going on in our minds and "focus in" on the realities of the Christian faith. This faith is grounded in the conviction that God has revealed himself fully in Jesus Christ and that by (1) actively coming to Jesus through worship and prayer, then (2) recommitting ourselves in trustful belief to God, and finally (3) forcefully throwing our worries onto God, we will be given peace and will experience relaxation.

1. "K" in Rippon's Selection (1787) in *The United Methodist Hymnal*.

> I think I can, I think I can, I think I can.
> —"THE LITTLE ENGINE THAT COULD"

CHAPTER 10

Further Steps Toward Relaxation

"Smile, you're almost home!" is a sign that appears at the Fox Island end of the bridge connecting that island with Gig Harbor, near Tacoma, Washington. I once spent several weeks in a cabin on that island. Each time I saw that sign I felt warm inside; it meant I was almost home. The cabin was less than a mile past the bridge.

"Smile, you're almost home" is now also a sign I place here, to remind Christian "relaxers" they are almost there. Once you have begun putting into practice the relaxation procedures suggested in the last chapters, you will have come a long way toward peace-filled living. This chapter will lead you into further ways that can help you deepen and lengthen the state of calm that, hopefully, you have come to cherish and desire. Included here are methods for deep muscle relaxation, ways to experience prolonged periods of calmness, techniques for reinstituting relaxation when tension arises, and directions for retaining awareness of your spiritual identity.

MAKE STRESS PREVENTION A WAY OF LIFE

Many programs for weight loss available today emphasize the truth that to keep the weight off one must learn a whole new pattern of eating. The same is true for relaxation. Unless you learn and practice a whole new pattern of being, the strain of daily living will eat away at you. Even your best intentions will not save you from returning to a stress-filled life.

So the first admonition I would give is: Practice! Practice! Practice! Don't forget the old maxim "Practice makes perfect." It does. Make relaxation exercises a part of every day and a new habit of peacefulness becomes ingrained.

A stop-smoking advertisement on television illustrated this accumulative effect of practice. It pictured a man with a chimpanzee hanging on his back. "This is the way you will feel the first week of the program," the voice stated. Then the scene switched to a monkey on the man's shoulder. "The second week you will feel less of an urge to smoke," the ad continued. The scene switched again. This time the man was holding the monkey in his arms, playing with it. The final scene showed the monkey jumping away. "After four weeks the monkey will be out of your life entirely," the announcer promised. Relaxation is like that. By practice, relaxation will become a habit. The monkey of stress will be off your back. You will have adopted a whole new style of life, and peaceful calm will be the rule, not the exception.

SELF-INDUCED DEEP MUSCLE RELAXATION

Below is a set of instructions for self-induced deep muscle relaxation. They can be read, followed, and memorized. While some people have found it valuable to team up with a friend who will guide them through the experience by reading the instructions aloud, in the final analysis these deep muscle relaxation steps are intended for individual use. The whole experience will take about thirty minutes and is well worth the time you spend. I recommend you practice this series of relaxation exercises daily.

As you will see, this particular experience of deep muscle relaxation is intended for Christians. It combines well-known mental procedures for relaxing those sources of tension deep within the muscles and ligaments of the body with the reaffirmation of biblical truths and the praying of prayers of release, acceptance, and restoration. In the best sense of the word, these instructions are a means of re-creation.

Sit down in a comfortable chair. Shut your eyes. Let your full weight settle down into the chair. Put both of your feet on the floor. Uncross your arms and let your hands rest on your lap. Cross your fingers, if you like, but do not grip them tensely together. Get comfortable.

Begin with the following *statements of affirmation*. (Say each one twice—either silently or aloud.)

"I am thine, O Lord, and thou art mine."

"I in my emptiness, thou in thy fullness."

"My heart, where the ocean of spirit meets the shore of self."

"This is the day that the Lord has made; I will rejoice and be glad in it."

"In returning and rest shall you be saved; in quietness and confidence shall be your strength."

"Be still and know that I am God."

"Thou wilt keep those in perfect peace whose mind is stayed on thee."

"For God so loved the world, that he gave his only begotten Son, that whoever believes in him should not perish, but have eternal life."

"Those that wait on the Lord shall renew their strength; they shall mount up with wings as eagles; they shall run and not be weary; they shall walk and not faint."

Here add or substitute scriptures or statements that have special meaning for you.

Next, engage in the following *prayers of release and acceptance*. (As you pray, breathe deeply; fill your lungs with air.)

With every prayer you exhale, release the evil in your life.

Let go your anger . . . your bitterness . . . your wrath . . . your selfishness . . . your anxiety . . . your tension . . . your apprehension . . . your worries . . . your distrust . . . your fears . . . your stress . . . your prejudgments . . . your distraction . . . your obsessions . . . your compulsions . . . your lust

. . . your sadness . . . your self-pity . . . your envy . . . your boredom.

Release these and all other evil and bad habits that handicap you. . . . Confess them and let them go out of your life with each exhaling of carbon dioxide from your lungs. . . . Think of them as the expunging of all spirits of evil from within yourself.

Now turn from those evils to address the unhealthiness of your body. Release it and let it go. Let go all the poison in your system . . . feel it flow out of your body through your fingertips . . . release your sickness . . . your disease . . . your pain . . . your infection . . . your high blood pressure . . . your overactive adrenal glands . . . your cancer . . . your tiredness . . . your overweight . . . your digestive problems . . . your headaches . . . whatever you suffer from, release it to God; let it leave you as you breathe deeply, breath upon breath.

After you have completed these prayers of release, pray the following prayers of acceptance:

With every breath you breathe in, accept calm . . . accept patience . . . accept joy . . . accept freedom . . . accept power . . . accept love . . . accept mercy . . . accept unselfishness . . . accept self-control . . . accept hope . . . accept insight . . . accept wit . . . accept wisdom . . . accept peace . . . accept focus . . . accept meaning . . . accept hope.

Follow these prayers of acceptance with prayers to accept good health . . . accept vitality . . . accept strength . . . accept energy . . . accept relaxation . . . accept healing . . . accept restoration . . . accept low blood pressure . . . accept good digestion . . . accept wholeness.

Feel yourself accepting as gifts from God all the goodness and health that come into your life. Continue to breathe deeply and enjoy these feelings of rest and restoration.

Now, turn to these *deep muscle relaxation exercises.*

Let each part of your body relax. As you breathe deeply, feel the relaxation move over all of your body. Quietly simmer down as you let your mind focus on one part of your body, then another. Begin with your head. Let all the tension in your scalp fade away. Imagine that the stress and strain you have been feeling in your head are melting away as smoothly as ice cream in a cone.

Feel the wrinkles on your forehead smooth out.

Untense your eyes; let them become pools of waveless waters.

Let your jaws drop; unclench your teeth; open your mouth a bit.

Feel your ears relax; let them become numb and less alert.

The tension of your head will flow down your cheeks and out your mouth; allow the relaxation to develop and increase.

Concentrate on the back of your neck; loosen these muscles.

Feel the tension in the front of the neck smooth out.

Next, move to your shoulders; experience the tension lessening and the strain of these muscles letting go.

Let your shoulders drop a little as they relax.

Feel the tension flowing off the shoulders and down the arms and out the fingers.

Concentrate on the joint where the arms connect to the shoulders; untense these muscles and ligaments.

Relax your arms . . . your biceps . . . your elbows . . . your forearms . . . your wrists . . . your hands . . . your fingers.

Let your arms hang limp. Feel the relaxation develop and deepen as tension leaves them and flows out of the tips of the fingers; experience tingling in your fingers as the tension leaves your body.

Turn now to a focus on the front of your torso; your chest, your breasts, your stomach, your groin. Allow the muscles down the front of your body to let go. Let your stomach stick out and your neck hang loose . . . feel the tension letting go.

Continuing to breathe deeply, and moving from one part of your body to another part of your body, ever so slowly:

Concentrate now on your back. Let the weight of life's burden lift. . . . Feel the tense muscles of your back smooth out and release. . . . Allow such tension as you might be experiencing to loosen up. . . . Feel the relaxation deepen and grow.

Pause and become aware of how calm and relaxed you are feeling. Experience the lack of tension in your head, neck, shoulders, arms, hands, stomach, front and back of your body. . . . Continue to breathe slowly and deeply.

Following a period of experiencing deep relaxation, go inside your body, starting with your mouth. Let your mouth relax . . . loosen your jaws . . . focus on your gums, your teeth, your tongue . . . feel the stress diminishing.

Focus on your throat . . . move down into your stomach . . . let your stomach relax . . . continue downward, into the upper and lower intestines . . . encourage these inner parts of your body to let go their strain and become restored to healthy function. . . . Let the restoration and relaxation grow.

Return to your face and concentrate on your nose. Untense

it. . . . Feel the air flow freely down through your windpipe. . . . Let the inside of your nose and the windpipe connecting to your lungs become free of mucus and contamination. . . . Feel the air enter your lungs as you breathe deeply and slowly. . . . Experience that air filling your lungs completely. . . . Let your chest protrude without inhibiting it. . . . Relax, do not force yourself. . . . Let the lungs inhale and exhale fully and completely as you continue to breathe deeply. . . .

Imagine the oxygen entering the bloodstream and energizing your body without any restraint or blockage. . . . Feel the lungs functioning freely without any effort. . . . Let your breathing be restored to its optimal state.

Now go deep inside your body and tell your heart to relax. Let the heart become free of all tension; let the heart muscles move in and out, automatically and effortlessly. Feel the heart being restored to calm, even, powerful, balanced function. . . . Let your heart become tension-free and structurally relaxed.

Once you have experienced the heart as being restored, concentrate on the flow of the blood out of the heart to the outermost parts of the body. . . . Let the arteries be open and the blood flow freely and powerfully. Think about the tips of your fingers . . . experience the blood as reaching the very ends of the fingertips; feel the warmth as the fingers heat up. Pause as you breathe deeply and slowly and concentrate on this experience.

Move now to focus on the ends of your toes. Feel the blood rush to the feet; let the toes warm up just as you did your fingertips. Let the blood reach the tips of your toes as all constriction and tension are released from the arteries. Feel the temperature of your feet increase as the blood vessels open up and the blood rushes to the very tips of the toes. . . .

The last place on the body to which blood is sent is the ears. Feel the lobes of the ears begin to get warmer as all inhibitions in arteries leading to the ears let go. Feel the ears get warm and the blood flow into them. . . .

Experience the continuous flow of blood from the heart to the fingertips, the ends of the toes, and the lobes of the ears. Imagine the return of the blood to the heart and its being pushed out again to the outermost parts of the body. Let yourself focus on this cycle and experience the warming of the fingers, the toes, and the ears. Take your time and breathe deeply. Let the body restore itself to an even, powerful, and unrestrained flow of blood to and from the outermost parts of the body and back.

Continue this relaxing of the inside of the body by focusing on the kidneys. Let them relax and be restored to healthy functioning.

Move to the liver. Let it be restored to working without stress or strain.

Concentrate on all other organs inside the body and instruct them to let go all that inhibits them from working as God intended them to work. Remove all poison and tightness that would handicap their health. Instruct the adrenal glands to calm down and become malleable and less inclined to secrete impulsively or quickly.

Return next to the muscles; focus on the thighs. Feel the tension in the thighs flow down and out through the legs and the toes. Let the thighs relax as you continue to breathe deeply. . . .

Let your concentration go to the knees. Release the knees from pain and strain. Let the ligaments and the muscles

surrounding the knees become loose. Continue downward
to the calves. Let the muscles on the front and back of the
calves smooth out and become relaxed. Feel your whole
body becoming calm and whole as you continue down the
body. . . .

Finally, concentrate on the ankles and feet. Feel all the
stress of the legs flow out the tips of the toes. Spread the toes
and feel the tingling of released strain as the muscles let go
all their tightness and their tension leaves the body. For several moments simply sit still, breathe deeply and slowly, and
enjoy the deep relaxation of all of your body. Feel the calm
and the relaxed exhilaration that sweep over you. . . .

Since you have relaxed the muscles and organs of the
body, concentrate next on the restoration of the bones to
healthy function. The mental rule of thumb for your thinking
is "down the muscles, up the bones."

Let the bones of the feet and ankles become loose. Feel
the strength and integrity of these bones as they are restored
by the release of the unneeded tension within them. . . .
Continue to breathe deeply and slowly. . . .

Move up to the shinbones and the knees. Let the tension
flow out of them; let their strength return. . . . Then concentrate on the thighs. . . . Next to the hips . . . Experience
them becoming whole again, without disease or stress.

Turn your attention to the backbone. Let the tail of the
backbone relax and all the tension of the spine pass away.
Move up the backbone disc by disc. Let the backbone
straighten upward and become whole. Where there are
pinched nerves, disjointed vertebrae, out-of-line adjustment—let them heal. Restore the backbone to its optimal
health and wholeness. . . .

Move up the backbone with every breath, one disc at a time. Allow for twenty-four steps from start to finish, from the tailbone to the skull. When you reach sixteen, stop and enjoy the feeling of comfort and relaxation in the lower part of your back. . . .

Then resume moving up the back, one step at a time with every breath you breathe, to the count of fifteen.

Now relax the ribs. Concentrate on each rib and instruct it to relax. Feel the connection of the ribs to the backbone; feel the healthiness of the ribs becoming restored. . . . Concentrate on each rib, one at a time. . . .

Let the relaxation continue up the backbone to the base of the neck. . . . When you reach the count of twenty, stop and concentrate on the shoulder bones . . . the arm bones . . . and finger bones. . . . Before, you relaxed the muscles; now, relax the bones. Feel your body's wholeness deepening with every breath you breathe.

Once you have relaxed the shoulders, arms, and fingers, return to the neck and continue relaxing the vertebrae into the skull itself. When you have reached the count of twenty-four, let the relaxation penetrate the whole cranium. Experience the strength and integrity of the whole neck and skull being restored and re-created. . . .

Now that you have finished relaxing the muscles and restoring the bones with relaxation, let the body "hum." Feel the messages going down the nerves of the backbone to the other parts of the body. Note how alive the body feels and how easily messages of sensation and movement flow up and down the body. . . . Continue to breathe deeply and slowly . . .

Note again the flow of the blood out of and into the heart. Reexperience the warmth of the body. Enjoy the complete relaxation of the body that results from following these instructions for deep muscle relaxation and restoration. . . .

End this experience by rededicating yourself to the will of God through repeating some of the statements of affirmation with which you began. These are as follows:

"I am thine, O Lord, and thou art mine."

"I in my emptiness, thou in thy fullness."

"My heart, where the ocean of spirit meets the shore of self."

"This is the day that the Lord has made; I will rejoice and be glad in it."

"In returning and rest shall you be saved; in quietness and confidence shall be your strength."

"Be still and know that I am God."

"Those that wait on the Lord shall renew their strength; they shall mount up with wings as eagles; they shall run and not be weary; they shall walk and not faint."

"Thou wilt keep those in perfect peace whose mind is stayed on thee."

People following these instructions and regularly practicing these exercises have it almost guaranteed that they will acquire a peaceful and calm stance to life that will not easily be shaken by circumstances. These are sure ways of preparing oneself for the onslaught of fortune and the stress of both expected and unforeseen threats to existence. Although such exercises as these will not guarantee freedom from stress, they will prevent needless anxiety and will help keep stress from becoming distress. They are the further steps in relaxation that those who are serious about handling stress triumphantly will find valuable.

RECOMMENDATIONS AND CAUTIONS

Relaxation exercises such as these do work; but a note of caution should be sounded. David Barlow of the Center on Stress and Anxiety at the State University of New York at Albany found in his research that relaxation therapy by itself was more effective than cognitive therapy or a combination of cognitive and relaxation therapy. The process I have outlined in this chapter could be thought of as just such a combination. It combines Christian faith with relaxation techniques. Barlow concluded that cognitive therapy may give people more information than they can use. I hope you will not find that true of the steps I have recommended. The failure of such a process as described in this chapter will occur only if one does not take seriously the acceptance and care of God, or if the faith becomes words that are said but not deeply experienced.

In contrast with Barlow's conclusions, Herbert Benson, of the Harvard Medical School, found faith to be a valuable adjunct to relaxation. Faith can help, he concluded in his book *Beyond the Relaxation Response*. He recommended that people include prayer with their relaxing exercises. Combining prayer and relaxation is what I have done in this chapter. Benson reported that people who repeated passages of scripture or the name of God were more inclined to experience stress reduction than those who did not. Nevertheless, once again, the ideas of faith that we have discussed in earlier chapters must not be substituted for the experience of faith. Faith must become very subjective and personal if we are to live peacefully and calmly.

Norman Cousins wrote a book entitled *The Biology of Hope*. In it he reported that he had acquired enough control over his blood pressure to lower it twenty points when he practiced his relaxation exercises. May you do half as well! It can be done—and faith can help.

Let us "practice the presence of God."
—BROTHER LAWRENCE

CHAPTER 11

Relaxation and Sanctification

Nobody wants stress. Everybody wants things to be perfect. "Perfection isn't unreachable," according to an ad in the *Los Angeles Times*. "It's closer than you think . . . in Valencia." Valencia is a picturesque suburb of Los Angeles on the edge of the high desert just north of the San Fernando Valley. Its landscape of rolling hills is dotted with rows of red clay–roofed, stucco houses nestled between the Santa Ana and San Gabriel mountains.

When you arrive in Valencia, you feel yourself embraced by the quintessential southern California life-style that has been touted as being only a little less than heavenly. Valencia has it all: hot tubs, swimming pools, tennis courts, Little League parks. It seems like Shangri-la. Within an hour you can be swimming in the ocean, walking a mountain trail, or searching for opals among desert rocks. Valencia even plays host to Magic Mountain, one of the area's best-known amusement parks.

Yet there is no magic to life in Valencia. Unfortunately for those who might believe everything they read in the newspaper, perfection has never been a place; persons long before and long since Ponce de León have discovered that. In our earthly life, absolute perfection is not an attainment, but an ideal—a state of mind and a way of living.

Those who drive north out of Los Angeles on the Golden State Freeway for about an hour will find Valencia, but they will not find perfection.

THE CALL TO HOLY LIVING

Christians have always known that Jesus' admonition to "be perfect" (Matthew 5:48) was a call to holy living wherever one's house was located or in whatever situation one was involved. In fact, Christians know that perfection, or sanctification, as it is usually known, can be impeded by living in such opulence as in the Valencias of this world. Wealth may, indeed, soften the blows of fortune that make life stressful. Without doubt, Valencia is a world away from the smog of the Los Angeles basin, from the traffic of the freeways, and from the demands of interacting cultures. Coming home to the ambience of Valencia will probably reduce blood pressure significantly; there is less to stress a person in Valencia than in Watts. But good fortune cannot easily be equated with holiness.

In fact, living in such upper-middle-class suburbs as Valencia often works in the opposite way. Frequently, when people are satisfied and successful, when they can retire to hot tubs and tennis courts, when they have more money than they need and more food than they want, they see no need for God. And "seeing a need for God" is the secret of holy living, or sanctification. Thus, it should come as no surprise that people who live in the Valencias of this world do not feel it necessary to relax themselves by using such religious models as I have described.

Jesus observed this truth. Seeing that rich people felt self-sufficient, Jesus concluded that it was "easier for a camel to crawl through the eye of a needle than for someone who is rich to enter the kingdom of God" (Matthew 19:24). Our present-day frame of reference tells us that a camel could never even come close to crawling through the eye of a needle, and therefore Jesus' message was that rich people could not even hope to reach God's kingdom.

However, the "needle" about which Jesus spoke was the entrance to sheepfolds. With great effort, camels can crawl through those doors and get in with the sheep. Rich people can get into the kingdom of God, but it is tough work. They do not routinely want to get into the kingdom of God; nor do they feel a need to reduce stress, because they do not experience much of it. When offered such a model for relaxation as I have described in this book, they might reply, "Thanks, but no thanks; we are getting along very well, thank you; who needs God's acceptance anyway?"

Sometimes, however, rich people take the opposite point of view. In contrast to those who have no need for God, they think that their possessions and their lack of frustration in life are signs that God has blessed them. God is not someone they discover by a need to be accepted in the midst of failure and discouragement. God becomes, instead, the one who has given them their riches and made life easy for them. They worship God *because* God rewards them. In their minds, lack of stress is a reward for their faithfulness, a blessing given to them by God. They would find my approach unnecessary because they experience little of the kind of stress about which I have written. Yet they would express a strong need for God. But he is a God who rewards them more than accepts them.

This type of rich person agrees with Yung Ho Cho, the pastor of the world's largest church, in Seoul, Korea. He has asserted that God has promised Christian people three blessings: health, wealth, and happiness. According to Reverend Cho, our being healthy, wealthy, and happy means that we have lived up to God's commands and he is blessing us accordingly. He might as well have said, "True Christians do not experience stress."

We all know that is not so. Things turn around, and misfortune strikes Christians as well as other people. However, those Christians who think that God tangibly rewards faithfulness still do not attempt to relax themselves by reexperiencing God's acceptance. Instead, they take stress as punishment and work all the harder at being good and doing good. They think that goodness pays off and that God will, once again, reward their behavior.

WORKS RIGHTEOUSNESS

In religious terms this attitude has been called "works righteousness." Whatever stress and the tension felt by those caught up in "works righteousness" results from their thinking that they can prove themselves to God by near-perfect obedience to his laws. And they trust that God will see them and bless them again as he did in the past. They strain to be perfect.

But this kind of perfection is impossible. Even St. Paul, in agony, admitted, "I do not understand my own actions. For I do not do what I want, but I do the very thing I hate" (Romans 7:15). If Paul could make this admission, I wager

most other Christians would agree with him when they are
truly honest with themselves.

A more mechanical illustration of Paul's observation that
being perfect is next to impossible can be seen in the Pageant
of the Masters, held annually at Laguna Beach, California.
Here famous paintings are reproduced life-size; indeed, the
people "in" the paintings are alive. Actors and actresses
stand motionless against backdrops replicating the back-
grounds of artists' original works. For several minutes they
must stand completely still, moving not so much as an
eyelash. They do so well at it that only spectators with
binoculars see even slight motion.

Yet those actors are not perfect. All of them have nights
when the audience sees them move. Try though they may,
their bodies simply will not hold still. Yet they continue to
aspire to be flawless in their performances. However, their
aspirations do not tyrannize them. They accept their frailty
and come back the next night to try again.

The pressure that comes from thinking that one can be
perfect and avoid all errors by making things go the way
they should each and every time can be very stressful. The
motto of works-righteous Christians is "Stress is God's
punishment of me; if I just work harder, God will bless me.
Things will work out if I do my part."

This pretense that one can please God by being perfect
may be a dead-end street just as surely as trying to hold
still for any length of time at the Pageant of the Masters is
next to impossible. Our human capacities to be perfect are
extremely deficient. Moreover, the difficulties we have in
controlling people and circumstances may be insurmountable. Murphy's Law that "if something can go wrong, it
will" is probably the rule rather than the exception in life.
Breakdown, failure, and stress are the norm.

Most important, God may not be in the business of rewarding goodness in the first place. In fact, Paul boldly stated this in Ephesians 2:8–9: "For by grace you have been saved through faith, and this is not your own doing; it is the gift of God—not the result of works, so that no one may boast."

That God may not be the "great rewarder" is not an easy truth to swallow. It has always been tempting to think pragmatically about God. To wit: we do our part and God will do his. That's the way it works in real life, so to speak. We assert ourselves, and we are paid for our effort. A day's pay for a day's work. It just feels like fair play to think God will deal with us in the same way. When tension rises, we should be able to work hard to make stress disappear. God should recognize our effort and reward us for it.

That God may work in any other way is difficult for us to understand. This was true in Paul's day. Eighth-century prophets such as Amos champion the theme that if Israel will just return to God, God will bless Israel and return it to its former glory. This theme can still be heard today. Some say that to believe that God rewards goodness is "the American way." In fact, it is a very common feeling that America is a country blessed by God because America has obeyed God in its customs and in its laws. When stress comes, many think that if we return to moral living, God will bless America. They have little patience with relaxation. Their motto is "When the going gets tough, the tough get going."

When such "tough going" does not immediately pay off, some people give up on God. In the Scriptures, Satan asserted that Job was this sort of person. When God depicted Job as a blameless and upright man, Satan answered, "Have you not put a fence around him and his house and all that he has, on every side? You have blessed the work of his hands, and his possessions have increased in the land. But stretch out your hand now, and touch all that he has, and he will curse you to your face" (Job 1:9–11). Had Job reacted like this, he would have ended up in the same place as the aforementioned rich people who see no need for God in the first place.

Job proved Satan wrong, however. He survived great calamity, and his faith was stronger after his misfortune than before. I am convinced that, through the centuries, innumerable Christians have joined Job in discovering that their faith was more dependent on "how they shouldered their crosses rather than how they wore their crowns," as the late Halford Luccock, professor of preaching at Yale Divinity School, once stated.

HUMAN FRAILTY—THE KEY TO PEACE

In the final analysis, however, our having to face stress may set us upon our one true road to holy living. Those who do not experience their own inadequacy may never master the model for relaxation that this book recommends. They may never come to know the limits of their human strength or the peace that can be theirs through faith in God's grace.

Paul stated this truth in a way that makes implicit the integral relationship of relaxation and sanctification: "There is therefore no condemnation for those who are in Christ Jesus. For the law of the Spirit of life in Christ Jesus has set you free from the law of sin and death" (Romans 8:1–2). These verses proclaim the same truth that Paul Tillich did when he said "You are accepted" by God. God accepts us. He does not condemn us. We belong to him in good times and bad; when we are worthy and when we transgress; when things go as planned and when they don't; when we plan well and work out our plan, but also when our plans blow up in our faces; when we succeed and when we fail. We are treasured by God. This is the knowledge that makes relaxation possible, that reduces our stress and strain. This is what keeps our stress from becoming distress. Paradoxically, it is God's love for us, and not our earnest striving, that makes sanctification, or holy living, possible.

A friend of mine tells a story that manifests this attitude of God toward us. His two grandchildren came to visit him at Christmastime. They had been having an argument about where to get their Christmas tree. One grandchild wanted to buy it at the supermarket; the other wanted to go into the woods and cut the tree down. Their parents were also split in their opinions. It was a two-to-two tie. The mother of one of the grandchildren said, "Maybe your grandfather will vote with you if you promise you will give him a dime." "He doesn't need money," the child replied. "Then tell him he can be your friend for life," she suggested. The child became silent. Then he answered, "Oh, that would never work; he's already that. And more." For the Christian, God is already a friend for life. And more. God does not need money or complete obedience. He accepts us. We can relax. We do not need to strain to be perfect.

GOD IS FOR US

Once again, St. Paul puts this truth in haunting terms when he states, "What then are we to say about these things? If God is for us, who is against us? . . . Who will bring a charge against God's elect? It is God who justifies. Who is to condemn? . . . Who will separate us from the love of Christ? Will hardship, or distress, or persecution, or famine, or nakedness, or peril, or sword? . . . No, in all these things we are more than conquerors through him who loved us. For I am convinced that neither death, nor life, nor angels, nor rulers, nor things present, nor things to come, nor powers, nor height, nor depth, nor anything else in all creation will be able to separate us from the love of God in Christ Jesus our Lord'' (Romans 31–39).

As the title of a book by Mark Trotter concludes, there is *Grace All the Way Home*. There is no stressful situation in the middle or along the side of life's road that can detour us from the love of God. He is with us all the way home.

A friend of mine recently recovered from throat cancer. He first suspected serious trouble when he experienced difficulty in swallowing his food. Physicians recommended radical surgery that involved the removal of certain lymph glands and ligaments. It was uncertain whether he would ever speak again. After the operation, his jaws were wired shut for several months, and he was fed through a straw. Fortunately his voice returned. Yet even today, he speaks out of the side of his mouth, and the muscles of his neck pull his face to the right. He recounted to me much of the pain and toil surrounding his illness, and yet assured me warmly, ''Newt, there has never been a day throughout all this travail that I have not been at peace. The grace of God has been sufficient.''

This grace of God is, indeed, the basis for Christian relaxation. That is the theme of this book. And, to add to our good fortune, God's grace is also the basis for Christian perfection and sanctification. Holy living can be grounded in knowing how to relax into God's grace. Let me explain.

TEACHING TERRORS TO SING

A beautiful quotation from the Chinese philosopher Quant states, "I must go away with my terrors until I have taught them to sing." This is an important starting point for Christians who would aspire to "relaxed sanctification" grounded in the love of God. Life holds many terrors, as Paul noted in the Romans passage quoted earlier and as can be seen in my friend's throat cancer. These terrors lead to much tension and stress. They are real. They cannot be minimized or explained away. They are more serious than those stresses about which I recommended we say, "It don't matter as much as I thought it did."

Yet for those who meditate sufficiently on the graceful presence of Almighty God in the midst of whatever happens to them, their terrors begin to "sing." They know that God is always there to love them, accept them, and strengthen them. They welcome the dawn, the afternoon, the evening, and the midnight of each day with the triumphant words of the Psalmist, "This is the day that the Lord has made; let us rejoice and be glad in it" (118:24). It is then that they become confident that "in everything, God works for good with those who love him, who are called according to his purpose" (Romans 8:28).

The terrors do not disappear, but Christians can relax because nothing can separate them from the love of God. Furthermore, God is with them, working for good in the midst of whatever terror may come.

CALLED ACCORDING TO GOD'S PURPOSE

After Christians have taught their terrors to sing, they invest themselves in trying to live devout and holy lives.

This may sound like bringing "works righteousness" in the back door. If God does not reward goodness and if Christians should relax themselves by relying on God's acceptance, why should they exert all this effort in holiness? After all, isn't it the very kind of frantic, frenetic, stressful activity we have been arguing against throughout this book? The answer to this last question is both yes and no. Yes, I disparaged attempts to prove ourselves pleasing to God. But, no, I have not thrown out the call of God to do good and to be good.

The Westminster Confession states that "the chief end of man [sic] is to serve God and enjoy him forever." To serve God means to do good and to be good. This is what Paul meant when he said that God works in all things for good with those who are "called according to his purpose." Those Christians who believe God rewards goodness have gotten this part right. Their only problem is that they think goodness comes before God's love rather than after it. The truth of the matter is that Christians are called to do good *because* God loves them, not in order for God to love them. And "working for good" in Paul's statement means to "work for God's will in life."

A well-known benediction speaks of how this call of God is at the heart of relaxation by stating, "May you have the peace that passes all understanding and the understanding that passes all peace." Christians who are committed to the call of God to holy living experience the peace and calm that makes life's stresses manageable at the same time that they willingly invite the stress that comes from trying to be the people God intended them to be.

This is a paradox. At one and the same time, Christians handle the stress of life by learning how to relax, yet they actually seek out stressful situations in which they can do good. Having come to know God's love for them, they can never be the same again. They are obligated to be God's servants even though they know God loves them whether they succeed or not. Yet they never cease trying to do his will.

Although not writing as a Christian, Hans Selye captures this truth in suggesting that one of the cardinal ways to a stress-free life is to come to know oneself and to be oneself. Having a mission in life can be one of the prime ways to focus one's energy and reduce confusion. According to Selye, once we have embarked on the mission of being who God intended us to be, we are like a pilot who, having left the ground in an airplane, must complete the flight plan. Christians know that being vigilant about opportunities to do good may seem to onlookers like inviting needless stress. But Christians know that they would be untrue to God's purpose for their lives if they became permanent "TV lounge lizards" who sought their own comfort only.

"Only Robinson Crusoe tried to get everything done by Friday" is an acidly humorous saying by an unknown author. It has a double meaning. Friday, in Daniel Defoe's novels, was the native islander who helped Crusoe survive a shipwreck; and with the passage of time, "Man Friday" has come to mean a jack-of-all-trades—often, one who gets stuck doing the lowlier tasks. But the saying also implies that people do not try to do by Friday in a given week every good thing that is to be done eventually. This is the very attitude with which Christians approach sanctification. They aspire to doing and being good but know their salvation is not dependent on it. God loves them in spite of their lack of achievement.

Thus, they are able to follow the admonition of St. Paul in his letter to the church at Galatia: "Brethren, let us not grow weary in well doing'' (6:9). This statement, like the Robinson Crusoe quote, has a double meaning. Relaxed Christians, who are aspiring to be holy, do not grow weary or despairing about their own failures or about whether God approves of them. At the same time, they do not get tired of trying to find ways and means to do and to be good.

Yet they know that not everything can be accomplished by Friday and, most importantly, they believe that God will bring them into his kingdom both despite their shortfalls and because of them. They are but God's helpers. They do not replace him. Although a well-known poem says that God, ''has no hands but our hands to do his work today,'' Christians know better. God is not entirely dependent on them. He is doing more than is being done by his followers. He wants Christians to join him in doing good, but his power far exceeds their efforts. Christians can relax. Although they should try hard to do God's will, they should never forget they are not entirely responsible for what happens.

It was said of Jesus that he ''went about doing good'' (Acts 10:38). His followers will try to do no less. That is what holy living means. Doing and being good does invite stress—but it is stress that is invited, not just tolerated. It is expressive, not oppressive, stress. And it is stress that results in peace and relaxation because it is grounded in the grace of God. Several more aspects of this relaxed stress of goodness need to be looked at.

GOODNESS IS NOT ALWAYS SUCCESSFUL

First, goodness is not always successful. It does not always work. Trying to be good will be doubly frustrating if we forget this. Back in the late 1950s I kicked over a fiery Ku Klux Klan cross thrown from a car in front of the church where I was pastor. Before I got home that night, my wife had received a phone call threatening that we would be killed if we did not leave town. Talk about stress! In this case, it was dangerous to be good. Although later the driver of that car apologized and asked for forgiveness, the night we spent after his phone call was almost sleepless! Our fears were hardly allayed by our knowing that the police chief in this town was himself a member of the Klan. I did a good thing, but it was not all that successful.

USA Today carried a story about a real estate agent, Donna Russell, who bought a split-level home and began taking in homeless women and children. The neighbors protested that her action violated the zoning laws. Russell reported that she was moved by her faith to help others and that she would challenge the law. If she failed to win a variance, Russell said, she would simply move to some other place because she was following God's orders to express her faith by taking people into her home for the rest of her life. Goodness did not mean success for her—at least, not in the short term.

GOODNESS WILL NOT CHANGE SOME THINGS

Second, we need to accept the truth that there are some things our goodness will not change. Relaxed do-gooders should pray daily the prayer of Alcoholics Anonymous: "God, grant me the serenity to accept the things I cannot change, the courage to change the things I can, and the wisdom to know the difference." A colleague of mine recently ended a thirty-year marriage by becoming involved in an adulterous affair. I confronted him with his immorality and told him of my deep disappointment with the cruel way in which he treated his wife and the callous manner in which he violated the standards of the institution where he worked. It has all been to no avail. He has not apologized or admitted his error—much less has he ended the affair. I need to quit obsessing about it and worrying over it. I am stressing myself needlessly. I have made my point. It is a good one. Now I need to admit that what's done is not going to change. I need to follow the Australian maxim "Been there, done that." I need to accept his behavior as something that won't change.

GOODNESS SHOULD NOT LEAD TO POMPOSITY

Third, Christians need to guard against pomposity as they go about doing good. Pomposity characterizes those who think they are better than they are. Pomposity leads to two errors: too much judgment and too little forgiveness. These might be understood as two sides of the same coin, the coin of pride. And pride is one of the seven deadly sins.

Judgment can be of two kinds. On the one hand, we can judge ourselves too gently while, on the other hand, we can judge others too harshly. Jesus' parable in Luke 18, about a Pharisee and a tax collector who went to the temple to pray, illustrates how tempting it can be to judge ourselves too gently. The Pharisee proclaimed, "I thank thee that I am not like other men, extortioners, unjust, adulterers, or even like this tax collector." Jesus compared such prideful hypocrisy with the remorse of the tax collector, who, "standing far off, would not even lift his eyes to heaven, but beat his breast, saying, 'God, be merciful to me a sinner.'" At this point, Jesus speaks to all of us who might claim to be free from sin by proclaiming that the tax collector "went down to his house justified rather than the other; for every one who exalts himself will be humbled, but he who humbles himself will be exalted'' (verses 10–14).

Jesus' statement should remind Christians that there is such a thing as ''good guilt.'' Christians need to be aware constantly of this temptation to compare themselves to others and claim they are perfect. They should take great care in the disdain with which they look on others who (they think) might not be as good as they are. All humans are equal at the foot of the cross. Christians should not comfort themselves by judging others too harshly. They, too, are forgiven sinners, in continuing need of God's love and forgiveness. A counselor in a church told me about a homosexual client who said he did not go to church anymore because, whenever he went, congregants judged him and made him feel like a sinner. This counselor answered wisely. He said, ''Welcome to the crowd. They make me feel that way, too. We all are sinners—in one way or another. Come back to church with me.'' This counselor's reply reflected good guilt.

GOODNESS ALWAYS INCLUDES FORGIVENESS

It is hard to forgive, particularly if one has been harmed by someone else's action. Failure to forgive is a prime cause of stress. When people have hurt us, we want to get even with them. If we are prevented from getting even, we get mad. We ruminate about how badly we have been hurt and about how unfair it is that we cannot pay them back for what they have done to us. We role-play what we will say and what we will do if we get the chance. This is needless and sinful stress. Forgiveness will relax us. Forgiveness is what following Jesus demands of us. Jesus told Peter that we should forgive 490 times; seventy times seven (Matthew 18:22). That means every time. There is no other way.

I remember a colleague who took a graduate student away from me. When the student became angered at one of my suggestions about his dissertation, he asked my colleague to take over as chair of his work. This she did without consulting me. She ignored the fact that the student and I had planned to publish his study together. For several years I planned ways to get back at her. I spent many hours contemplating evil. I hoped she would fail. If she had been fired, I would have rejoiced. Then one day I came to my senses. I realized my stress was sinful. I had not forgiven her. As long as I held the grudge, I would be failing to do what I knew Jesus called me to do. It was the hardest thing I ever did, but I did it.

Forgiveness is the name of the Christian game. It alone, above all other behaviors, is the most important way to be a relaxed and sanctified Christian.

So, I end this book where I began. Becoming relaxed is possible, and even probable, for Christians. Contrary to what many may believe, it is the highway to goodness and holy living. May it become true for you. I wish you well.

> Most people are intelligent—
> it is method that they lack.
> —FRIEDRICH NIETZSCHE

CHAPTER 12

When to Start Relaxing? Today!

"Insight doesn't heal." That saying among counselors acknowledges that what most people lack is not intelligence. People often *know* better than they *do*. They have intelligence and they have insight, but neither intelligence nor insight nor the two in tandem is enough to get people off their duffs. Becoming relaxed takes more than intellectual ability and knowledge, more than intelligence and insight. Relaxation takes action—or a "method," as Nietzsche stated.

An old, anonymous poem points out the danger of intelligence without method. It goes like this:

The sermon now ended, each turned and descended.
The eels went on eeling, the peels went on peeling.
Much delighted were they, but preferred the old way.

Someone might ask, "Why do people prefer the old way?" There are two possible answers to this question. The first is that the old way, no matter how uncomfortable, is familiar. And the familiar is, for most of us, always preferable to the unknown. Most of us know we want to stop being stressed out. We are far less clear about what we want to put in the place of stress, amazing though that may sound.

There is risk in the new and the unknown. The risk is, of course, that the new may not work. David Barlow in his research on stress found that in some people, relaxation exercises provoked anxiety and panic attacks. Appallingly, their stress increased; the opposite of calm and peace occurred. This may happen when we feel most in need of a quick fix. When change does not occur as fast as we had hoped, we tend to suffer from a rebound effect of stress.

However, the risk is far greater that the new way *may* work and that this success will require a whole host of changes that we had never intended. Eric Berne, the founder of transactional analysis, pointed out this danger. He suggested that most of us want to know how to live with less pain the old life we've been living. Only rarely are we motivated to change our whole style of life. We all develop "programs" to fill the time and to obtain recognition and approval. We continue to practice even our bad habits, such as hypertension and stress addiction, because they paid off (in at least some fashion) in the past. We fear the new because we don't know if it will be any better than the old, and it may require more change than we are willing or able to take in stride.

The second reason that we "prefer the old way" is that change is hard work. As William James, probably the best-known American psychologist, wrote in the early 1900s, habits are difficult to change. Much effort and practice are required. Becoming a relaxed, peace-filled, calm person when we have become habituated to stress will require intentional, consistent, and repeated effort on our part. It will not happen easily or without our commitment to act—over and over again.

Ray Bradbury's stage play *The Wonderful White Ice Cream Suit* illustrates the kind of effort that is required for real change to occur. Both method and action are necessary. Five poor, dream-filled Hispanic men see a white ice cream vendor's suit on display in a clothing store window. They pool their funds and buy it. It is the opposite of their life conditions. It stands for all their dreams and hopes. Then they agree that, since there is only one suit and there are five men to wear it, they will allow each man to wear the suit for one day at a time. The play is the delightful account of how the ''wonderful white ice cream suit'' changed each man's life. Once the suit was put on, each man began to create a unique reality of his own. As Nietzsche would say, they each had a ''method,'' and they wasted no time in putting it to work.

There is no time like the present to try on the ''relaxation suit'' and let stress reduction change your life. The answer to the question of ''When to begin relaxing?'' is ''Now!''— no sooner, no later. Give yourself permission to make a U-turn and begin relaxing this very moment. Better still, put this book down. Stop reading and give yourself permission to practice the exercises described in chapter 7. If you have forgotten them, turn back to page 73 and refresh your memory. Try them out for size; see if they don't work for you.

On a flight I took to Seattle the pilot said, ''Look out to

the right side of the airplane. You can see Lake Tahoe and the Sierra Nevada mountains. You better look now, because the next hundred miles will be cloudy and overcast. You will be able to see little if anything." As your pilot, I might say, "Learn *now* how to relax, because the next part of your life may be rough, rocky, and tumultuous. You will need your strength. Things could get worse. Knowing how to relax in the midst of the storm may turn out to be a valuable skill you will be glad you have."

In fact, my own practice is to go through most of my relaxing exercises while I am jogging—just to illustrate to myself the importance of learning how to relax during the very moments I am being most active. This procedure continues to impress on me the importance of going about my daily work with "manageable tension and no more." As I noted in Chapter 5 in quoting Mainelli's letter, life is lived in the face of everyday demands. That is where we must learn to relax. We need to be able to remain calm Monday to Friday much more than we need to attend weekend retreats in idyllic settings or sleep for twelve hours straight.

One last comment is in order: Don't expect that you will change overnight. Don't become discouraged if you fall back into your old pattern of hypertension and stress addiction. However, over the next month you should expect slow, but sure, progress. The old stress habits should change. You should find yourself becoming overstressed less often. When stress occurs, it should last for a shorter time. And the feelings of agitation should be less intense. Stated positively, you should experience calmness and peace more often—even in the midst of frustration and tension. Such beneficent states should last for longer periods and should feel deeper and more pervasive when they occur.

Stick with it. Don't give up. As Jack LaLanne says in his television ads, "If I can do it, so can you; don't give up, gang!" I would add, "Don't give up—for your own sake! . . . for God's sake!"

Scoring Key
Life Event Checklist

ALEC Scoring Key (in Life Change Units)*

Life Events	Full Score	.7	.3
1. death of spouse	125	88	38
2. institutionalization	82	57	25
3. death of a close family member	67	47	20
4. personal injury, still problem	67	47	20
5. personal illness, still problem	67	47	20
6. getting a divorce	64	45	19
7. being fired from work	64	45	19
8. personal injury, not a problem now	57	40	17
9. personal illness, not a problem now	57	40	17
10. major change in financial state	56	39	17
11. retirement	55	39	17
12. marital separation	54	38	16
13. being physically or sexually abused	54	38	16
14. getting married	50	35	15
15. death of a close friend	50	35	15
16. change to a family member	47	33	14
17. change in gratifying activities	46	32	14
18. major change in sexual behavior	45	31	13
19. change in work responsibilities	43	30	13
20. change in residence	43	30	13
21. changing to different line of work	41	29	12
22. pregnancy	40	28	12
23. spouse starting or stopping work	40	28	12
24. change in living conditions	40	28	12
25. marital reconciliation	39	27	12
26. major business readjustment	39	27	12
27. major change in social activities	38	27	11

*Full Score if event happened within past year, .7 if event occurred 1-5 years ago, .3 score if event occurred over 5 years ago.

28. major increase in family arguments	35	25	11
29. losing driver's license	34	24	10
30. change in number of people in home	33	23	10
31. reaching sixty-five years of age	32	22	10
32. reaching seventy years of age	31	22	9
33. major in-law troubles	29	20	9
34. change in working conditions	28	20	8
35. major troubles with the boss	28	20	8
36. holidays, anniversaries spent alone	28	20	8
37. outstanding personal achievement	28	20	8
38. major revision of personal habits	24	17	7

Childhood or adolescence:

	.1
39. unwed pregnancy	10
40. divorce of parents	9
41. marital separation of parents	9
42. having a visible physical deformity	8
43. becoming involved with alcohol or drugs	8
44. jail sentence of a parent	8
45. discovery of being adopted	7
46. major change in acceptance by childhood peers	6
47. marriage of parent to a stepparent	6
48. pregnancy in an unwed teenage sister	6
49. failure of a grade in school	6
50. frequently changing schools	5

About the Author

H. Newton Malony is a Christian clinical psychologist who is Professor and Director of Programs in the Integration of Psychology and Theology in the Graduate School of Psychology, Fuller Theological Seminary, Pasadena, California. He is an ordained United Methodist minister of the Pacific-Southwest Conference of the United Methodist Church. He has authored and edited numerous books and articles concerning the psychology of religion. He works daily with troubled persons who are seeking to reduce the stress in their lives and continues to reflect on his own experience toward the end that he may become a faithful servant of God in a pressured world.

FINDING THE STRENGTH WE ALL POSSESS...

with Ballantine Books